A FIGHT WORTH HAVING

DEFEATING THE 8 GIANTS
STOPPING YOU FROM A LIFE OF VICTORY

DELAVAGO SCRUGGS

A Fight Worth Having
Defeating the 8 Giants Stopping You From a Life of Victory

Published by
Kingdom Publishing, LLC
Odenton, Maryland, U.S.A.

Printed in the U.S.A.

Library of Congress Control Number: 2021901354

Paperback ISBN: 978-1-947741-61-4
E-book ISBN: 978-1-947741-62-1

Dedication & Acknowledgements

To **Dr. Shirley Faye Yarnall,** the former Dean of the Literature Department at American University in Washington DC. She was my creative writing teacher when I was a student there. She was the first person in my life to tell me that I had "the gift of writing." Her affirmation made an indelible impression upon my life that exists to this very day.

To **Archbishop Alfred A. Owens, Jr.** and **Co-Pastor Susie Owens,** who took me in at the tender age of 11, and for the next 5 years poured the Christian foundation in my life. Countless doors of opportunities and blessings came my way because of their love and generosity, for which I'm eternally grateful.

To **Dr. Alma "Sugar" Moseley Belcher**... what can I say about her?!? She was the one person who, when the world had given up on me, threw me a lifeline, and loved me up and out of a horrible pit. She loved me fiercely until Christ was formed in me. She travailed for me throughout the course of time. Mother Belcher has taken her wings and flown to the eternal resting place. She's gone but will never be forgotten.

To my best friend **Wayne Johnson**, and his wife **Tonya**... I love you both so much. Wayne, you have been a friend that has stuck closer than a brother. You both have been rock steady anchors in my life, through trials and triumphs, for 25+ years. I am grateful to have you in my life.

To **Apostle Antonio Palmer** and **Pastor Barbara Palmer,** my Pastors, whom I love dearly. I cherish our multidimensional, covenant relationship; our paths joined at the appropriate and appointed time. God did a marvelous thing in my eyes leading the Scruggs family to you both. Words are inadequate. You two are platinum level saints of God in your care, service and love for the people of God. I wish I could tell the world of the gift you two are.

To the **Kingdom Celebration Center**, my beloved church family... I appreciate all of you so much! Thank you for receiving me, Pastor Aretha, Jonothan, Joelle and Lailani... I love you more than words could ever say.

To **Velvita Rose Alexander (Scruggs)**, my mother, whom I love deeply. You have weathered so much in life... I thank God for keeping you until we could reconnect again. Love has washed away the old things, and has made room for the new between us, for which I am eternally grateful.

To **Desi, Veronne,** and **Spring**, my brothers and sister... I love each of you dearly. We have been through many trials as a family, but the faithfulness of God is displayed in that we have found each other again. The joy I have in my heart to have you all back in my life... priceless.

To our **Tribe—the Wilkersons, the Browns, the Williams,** and **the Butlers**, my kingdom-covenant brothers and sisters who have given me love, support, strength and consistency for many years... I love, appreciate and honor each of you.

To **Oscar Ward**, my oldest friend, who was my co-defendant and dorm-mate in the maximum-security wing of the Lorton Penitentiary of Virginia (aka "the country"), where we spent 5 years inside the lockdown unit nicknamed "The House of Pain." I cherish our 45 years of friendship. Like you, I look back and marvel from whence the Lord has brought us!

To **Alexis, Amelia, Alexondra, Jonothan**, and **Joelle**, my children. You all mean the world to me and bring me such joy. I am filled with gratitude that God chose me to be your Dad. Time nor distance will never remove the love in my heart for you and my grandchildren.

And last, but certainly not least...

To **Aretha,** my wife... my "Sugar!" I have said this more times than I can count, and it will be what I repeat until I am no more. David said in Psalm 41:11, *"By this I know that Thou favourest me, because mine enemy doth not triumph over me."* But I say, by you being in my life, I know the Lord favors me! You are my sign of how much God loves and favors me. You mean the world to me. *"You're Still the ONE!"* and always will be.

FOREWORD

Although retired now, after over thirty-three years practicing as a Clinical Psychologist, I have witnessed the mental, emotional, and spiritual suffering of hundreds of broken people. Many of these individuals had experienced some type of traumatic event. For some, the trauma occurred early in their life. For others, the trauma occurred in adulthood. Some were caught off guard, while others endured a chronic history of abuse. As a therapist, I have had the privilege to walk alongside numerous persons as they labored to regain psychological equilibrium. I observed in my work with wounded people is a common thread of two basic practices: acknowledging that they had a problem and the willingness to face that problem. These brave souls labored to heal despite fears of the known and the anxieties of the unknown. Their goal? To regain or attain a fulfilling and more successful life.

As human beings, we are triune in nature, intricately connected mind, body, and soul. What impacts one area of our being affects the other parts of ourselves. With this understanding, the process of becoming whole again requires engaging these three parts of our nature. To think or say, I am going to get my healing sounds simple enough. The reality is that the work of restoration is a gradual process. It is one of the most difficult challenges we face as humans. The good news? All things are possible if we are working with the right tools. You will discover as you read this soul and spirit searching book that having the right biblical tools are essential.

When we find ourselves caught up in an inner battle, we may also feel stuck in bondage. Spiritually speaking, we may feel opposition coming from many directions as if doing battle with a spiritual or demonic giant. Prophet Delavago Scruggs writes about our "giant" being that something that stops us from living a fulfilling and victorious life in Christ. It may be something that seems so big and powerful it renders us incapable or helpless to fight. Have you felt this way? Do you feel your soul and spirit are losing the fight? Do you feel bound? Do you desire to be released from the bondage that you have been fighting against for years or even decades?

Prophet Delavago Scruggs offers a biblically based blueprint for us to become victorious in our spiritual battles. If you are exhausted or feeling hopeless because of repeatedly fighting the same spiritual or demonic "giants", over and over again—and are finally ready to start on a course to free yourself from bondage, then you must read and then ingest "A Fight Worth Having" into your spirit.

As the title suggests, "A Fight Worth Having" is raw, real, honest and edifying. Although I must warn you, if you are up to the challenge of facing, fighting and defeating what Prophet Scruggs refers to as the "giants" in your life, this book will give you spiritual tools to face and defeat them. Get ready to more clearly see how to effectively navigate this maze on your journey to attain victorious living.

Let me say here, I have had the privilege of interacting with Prophet Delavago Scruggs. While we have taken different paths, reside in different geographical locations, and only intermittently connected over the many years, I have a personal knowledge of his flight from a defeatist mind-set to a mind-set of victory. In his book, "A Fight Worth Having," Prophet Scruggs courageously put his years of struggle with his "giants" on full display for the reader to see and glean from. His teachings are informed by his theological and pastoral training, as well as, his life's journey, in general. While the primary focus is spiritual, he has wisely weaved together the intricate connection of mind, body, and spirit. This awareness is necessary for a deeper and enduring transformation. As a minister, as well as a psychologist, I find this a refreshing reveal of Prophet Scruggs' insightfulness.

I know for myself the positive and transformative impact of this book. When I was asked to write the "Forward" for this book, I did not feel worthy of such an honor. I was keenly aware of my own spiritual struggles triggered by painful experiences and disappointments. Indeed, I was in the midst of a battle with my own giants. I didn't refer to the opponent I was facing as a giant. Nevertheless, I was engaged in a spiritual fight. I felt I was losing the battle.

Soon after I delved into this book, I came to the revelation that there was more to the request to pen this "Forward". Prophet Scruggs and I were unaware of this at first. This was not an intellectual exercise of simply reading for content. It was spiritual. The message was specific to me. I now believe that God had intended all along to use the principles laid out in this book to also minister to me. First, I had to read it. Almost immediately I sensed the emergence of a spiritual breakthrough. I felt strengthening within my soul and spirit. I was not to surrender in my personal battle. I was to continue until I was victorious. I would get the victory. This was a God-promise. I was having an encounter with God both revelatory and profoundly transformative. I received an unexpected blessing simply by carrying out my assignment.

I am confident that this book will also minister to your need. You will be encouraged with the hope-filled knowledge and wisdom that no matter where you are in your spiritual journey, if you are facing and fighting giants, "it's a fight worth having!" The "spoils" of victory are waiting for you to claim.

Be Blessed!

Dr. Deborah Nunnally-Blowe, Ph.D.
Clinical Psychologist (Retired)
Ordained Minister

Prologue

Do you have the courage to look at Scripture objectively, and explore what is actually there with an openness to have the truth revealed to you, rather than seeing only what you have always been taught or what has always been preached in your hearing?

What I am about to say is not meant to be condescending, but in truth, there are many people who have never heard or read prophetic teaching, preaching or writings. This book is indeed a prophetic and deliverance revelation, written especially for those seeking to slay their personal giants.

Back in May and June of 2018, I preached a two-part message at my home church (Kingdom Celebration Center) entitled, *"You Must Make Adjustments in This New Season."*

The Lord wanted me to provoke each listener with this revelation: *"If we are to enjoy the land of promise, the land of abundance, the land of personal victories, we will need to make adjustments in the new season that God is leading us into..."*

The Word of the Lord pricked all of our hearts, so much so that at the conclusion of the 2nd message, my pastor stood before the church and said, "Prophet, you need to make this message a book!" and the people there chimed-in affirmingly in agreement.

Over the next two years, those who were present, as well as those who watched the sermon later, shared with me how much the sermon impacted them, and many encouraged me with their written feedback...

The most important takeaways for me were:
- *Settle yourself; the suddenlies of God are the exception, the rule of God is little by little (my favorite scripture)*
- *The house of God is distinguished by consistency*
- *Giants are an indicator that you are in the promised land*

—Pastor Akhirah Padilla

"The second sermon is so prophetic to where we are today. The word was true back then but now it exudes our reality in plain sight! It's so on point that it amazes me. Prophet said that "KCC is going to turn the region upside down," and with everything that's been going on during the pandemic and being able to see the behind the scenes, it's truly just the beginning of that prophecy. Major events have happened through our Apostle and First Lady that have shaken a lot of people and things up. Prophet also said that "the Lord wants to do something, and not within the four walls." That's literally all that we've done as a church since the pandemic started. "This cannot be church as usual," Prophet said. There is nothing that is the same about KCC from this sermon to now.

—Destini Joyce

The "7-ites" message is a war cry to the body of Christ, reminiscent of the 7 letters John the revelator wrote to the 7 churches. Each letter put a spotlight on the mindset or culture of the particular church. Likewise, the message provokes the individual believer to self-examination, and challenges the body of Christ to search within to evaluate areas of failure and brokenness. Each giant represents the struggles the believer faces as they attempt to apprehend the fullness of the promises of God. "Giants in the land are an indicator that we are close to the promise."

- *The "-ites" are big and intimidating.*
- *The "-ites" are BOLD and ugly.*
- *The "-ites" seem powerful and unstoppable.*

And each one will cause the believer to evaluate the maturity of their faith. But the "Ites" have a purpose. They each are strongholds. These can only be defeated with the authority and audacity of the most high God- Yahweh. Once defeated, we see ourselves as stronger warriors for the Kingdom. They cause us to be better, more mature, and more "faith filled" believers.

—Minister Erica Brown

I thought it was impactful. It touched on issues that everyone has been through or is currently going through. Not only did it point the giants out but gave weapons to destroy the giant. I also like the inclusion of real-life testimony. It made the message more personal.

There were so many nuggets, but the two that stood out to me were: "little by little" and warring against the giant of fear. It's in daily obedience of the little by little that builds us up to who God is calling us to be. We often see people like the Ravi's of the world from a biblical perspective and don't consider the daily obedience it took to get there. The same thing in regard to fitness; it took Dwayne Johnson's obedience in the little by little to achieve his present level of fitness.

The pursuit for academic advancement and overcoming fear spoke to me. The odds appeared to be stacked against you, but you pressed beyond it all. Hearing your testimony may have reignited me to get back on track to learn coding and programing. One of the things that the sermon highlighted for me is the comfort in fear that people endure until they no longer realize that it's fear holding them back.

The practical steps to take and the spiritual steps to take in vanquishing the giants we face was very good. Marrying the practical with the spiritual will do great things for whoever reads through the book.

—Corey Wilkerson

The sermon about the "-ites" or giants was impactful and full of practical wisdom. The Old Testament can be hard to understand because of the language, but when you have the words put into natural terms that we use and see in operation today, it makes a difference. The most important takeaway for me is how the giants represent the struggles that we have in our personal lives, and how the giants are working in us to hinder others from getting their blessing.

—Min. Charlene Hawkins

"Many need to know who they are, what they are, why they are and where they are in relation to one or more of these '-Ites' (giants).
As I was writing this part, I was still listening to the sermon and you said at the moment of my writing, "Giants are an indicator that you are right there..." You said, "Just beyond that giant ("-ite"), My promise

is there." That is what the reader of your book will take from this: to know and be pricked in their heart and convicted in spirit that they are that Giant at that moment, or that they are being attacked by that Giant at that time. This is a time that the reader will see what they have not been understanding about themselves or questioning their circle or family.

—Joanne McMillian

"I loved the message! What I loved most is when you spoke on "The Hittite Giant: The Giant of Terror and Fear." I'm the type of person that struggles with fear; I have fear when it comes to the known and the unknown. I have normal fears like everyone else but I'm more fearful than I should be, so I wrote down the scripture 2 Timothy 1:7 and memorized it so that I can speak it into the atmosphere and ease my heart, my mind, and my body!"

—Joelle Scruggs

The sermon I preached those two Sundays in 2018 is the foundation of this book. And now, through the Holy Spirit, amplification of those foundational truths lay right here at your fingertips. I must also forewarn you that threads of transparency about my life are also laid out throughout this book, just as it was throughout the sermon, and some of it may be offensive to you. If transparency and honesty about the faults and failures of men and women of God offend or disgust you, this book may not be for you; in fact, you may want to go ahead and put it down.

But before you go, please indulge me a moment to remind you of a few offensive stories throughout the Bible, just in case you may not know or remember. The first five books were penned by Moses, who was a murderer. Most of the Psalms were by written by David, who was a murderer and adulterer. Solomon wrote two books of the Bible, but during the last years of his life, he went after foreign gods. Paul wrote 13 books of the Bible and was said to have been responsible for the stoning of hundreds of Christians before his conversion. James was Jesus's half-brother and although he grew up in the same house with Him, he didn't even believe in Jesus until after the resurrection. Peter wrote 2 books of the New Testament but denied Christ 3 times before becoming the leader of the earlier church.

If you're still here, allow me to share a few more things that you may or may not know about men and women of God whose faults and failures may be many, but are still used mightily by Him, as long as they remain vessels of clay in His hand:

- If you were to rip out all the books of the Bible written by murderers and failures, you would lose much of the Old Testament, and most of the New Testament
- The Bible includes books written by people who didn't even walk with God by the end of their lives, yet their writings are still part of the holy writ, and read by millions from generation to generation, in order to learn how to walk with God.
- Just because someone fails in life doesn't mean that they aren't deserving of honor for the blessings that their lives provided for the world at some point of their journey.
- If we held the writers of the Holy Bible to the same standard that we hold government leaders, entrepreneurs, sports figures and entertainers and pioneers, I'm not sure any of us would continue to read it.
- No matter how much you've failed in your personal world, it's never too late to become a "world changer" from God's perspective.

I said all this to say that God appoints and anoints ordinary, broken people who are surrendered in His hand… and I'm one of them. I pray that my openness and transparency edifies and encourages you no matter where you are in your journey and fight for personal deliverance and victory against the giants in your life.

There are a few more things I want to point out as we begin. Let's look at the very first mention of giants in the Bible, found in Genesis 6:4: *"There were giants in the earth in those days; and also after that, when the sons of God came in unto the daughters of men, and they bare children to them, the same became mighty men which were of old, men of renown."*

The first thing to note is that giants have been here since the beginning. They were physically imposing human beings because they were the offspring of spiritually demonic beings and humanity. But here's what I need you to catch: it says that giants were in the land in those days *and thereafter...* meaning, they never went away!

There were giants to conquer then, and there are giants to conquer now, in this life! And even when you and I conquer our giants, others will still be in a fight with theirs; and giants will still be here long after. No matter who you are, no matter what heights you reach in life and/or ministry, there are always giants for you to fight, conquer and overcome!

My journey to living a life of victory against giants entails what I have learned in over 40 years of ministry... from preaching in 25 states across this country... from large urban cities to small rural places, from mega congregations of thousands to small storefronts... as well as all the "life" that happened in between.

The message that I preached which led to the writing of this book can be summed up in a quote by President Theodore Roosevelt: *"Nothing in the world is worth having or worth doing unless it means effort, pain, and difficulty... I have never in my life envied a human being who led an easy life. I have envied a great many people who led difficult lives and led them well."*

I love this quote for so many reasons, but primarily because it sums up my life. To that end, please know that I will not be guilty of attempting to romanticize these giants for literary purposes. Spiritual warfare and sincere efforts to be free and delivered from domination from these giants is gut-wrenching for those who are in the fight. For those of you reading this book who are in the midst of the fight of your life, know this: you can do this... you can defeat your giants and live a victorious life in your land of promise! May the Lord's blessings be multiplied to you.

—**Prophet Delavago Scruggs**

Table of Content

Dedication and Acknowledgements i

Foreword v

Prologue ix

Introduction 1

Chapter 1 The Baggage of Egypt 15

Chapter 2 In War, There Must be Adversaries 29

Chapter 3 The Canaanite Giant 39

Chapter 4 The Hittite Giant 53

Chapter 5 The Hivite Giant 65

Chapter 6 The Perizzite Giant 77

Chapter 7 The Girgashite Giant 85

Chapter 8 The Amorite Giant 93

Chapter 9 The Jebusite Giant 99

Chapter 10 The Self-Destructive Giant 105

Chapter 11 Conclusion 113

Chapter 12 Epilogue 127

Bibliography 134

Author's Page 137

I must become an adversary to my adversaries.

Introduction

THE DIVINE PRINCIPLE OF LITTLE BY LITTLE

*"And the Lord your God will drive out those nations before you **little by little;** you will be unable to destroy them at once, lest the beasts of the field become too numerous for you."* —Deuteronomy 7:22

A "principle" can be defined as: *a moral rule or belief that helps you know what is right and wrong and that influences your actions; a basic truth or theory; an idea that forms the basis of something.* (Merriam-Webster)

The scripture above introduces us to a divine principle, given from the Lord Himself to His people, that explains how they will be victorious in the land He promised them. This word from the Lord--this principle--if understood, followed and obeyed, would lead them to experiencing victory by His mighty power. It is the divine principle of *"little by little."*

This principle was not popular amongst the children of Israel, and it's certainly not popular amongst us believers today. And why is that? Because we live in a culture where instant gratification is the desire of far too many believers and unbelievers alike.

Imagine the children of Israel hearing that there are giants in the land that had been promised to them, and they would be driven out "suddenly." I imagine many of them were thinking, "Wait a minute... You are the God of the supernatural... You are the God of the miraculous... You are Jehovah Jireh (the Lord who provides) ... why don't You just snap Your fingers and cause these giants to disappear? Can't you hit them with some large boulders and we'll take care of the clean up after You knock them dead?" But as you can see, it didn't work that way for them, which means it won't work that way for us either.

So if you are ready to be set free from the bondage that giants have ensnared you in, if you are ready to be set free from *giant* issues, *giant* struggles, *giant* problems that have plagued your life, I'm here to tell you that it will be a process. But It won't be just any

2

kind of process, neither will it be a self-prescribed process; it will be a *God-ordained* process. He works through processes, and you and I must trust Him in the process.

Last year I was led to preach a sermon entitled, *"Understanding the Value of the Process."* One of the points I shared is that relationship with the Lord teaches us that He uses 'process' to develop us; and 'process' does not feel good most of the time. In fact, 'process' often feels very uncomfortable; it even hurts. But if you walk with Him long enough, you will come to know this divine truth as well: there is no progress without process.

Often, what feels to us like an ongoing battle is actually God taking us through His process of little by little. The Apostle Paul calls it "a light and temporary affliction" (2 Cor 4:17). No matter how long the process lasts, from God's perspective, it's just for a moment. This moment is a part of His process for you, and it's working for your good! Not only is it working for you, it's working *in* you an exceeding and eternal weight of glory! Little by little has eternal benefits!

For example, one of the main spiritual benefits gained through God's process of little by little is the fruit of patience. When God wants to develop patience in us, He places us in situations that require patience from us, so that, little by little, we can develop the spiritual muscles needed to endure life's weightier circumstances and battles, which become a part of our process of growth and maturity.

I feel the need to stop and encourage you right here. Just as your life is more than your failures, your mistakes, your blown opportunities, your failed marriage, your child born out of wedlock, and your lapses in judgement, your life is definitely more than what is happening to you right now. Just remind yourself that it's temporary. Your temporary setback will eventually yield to His timeless sovereignty IF you submit and obey the Word of the Lord that you are hearing Him speak to you right now.

A WILLINGNESS TO CHANGE

In order to further understand and embrace God's divine principle of "little by little," you must have an understanding that our steps are ordered by the Lord (Psalm 37:23). This means all of our steps (and stops) are divinely orchestrated by Him; it's a part of His process to develop and mature us.

A lot of you know and quote that scripture by heart, but the real challenge for many of you reading this right now is that you fight the steps He orders for you because you hate the changes they require from you. But here's the revelation He wants you to get and receive: His ordered steps are a part of His divine process for you, but you cannot walk in His ordered steps unless you **yield to change!** Your mindset must change concerning *how* He orders your steps! He requires us to change not only our mindsets, but our hearts, our ways, and our behavior. If we are not willing to change, we will not internalize His principle of little by little, and ultimately, we will abort God's process for us.

The concept of change is nothing new; change happens all around us all the time; change is a constant in today's society, impacting both our personal and professional lives. And these changes require adjustments on our part; sometimes we need to make small adjustments, and at other times, we need to make huge, significant adjustments.

And then there's a type of change where I believe God's principle of "little by little" applies the most and yields the greatest value for us… it's the type of change that doesn't happen around us, nor to us, but **in** us… it's what I call *transformational change.*

Transformational change happens when God allows His Holy Spirit to facilitate an inward change within. This is the most challenging type of change because it's an individual, personal change, that we often have to walk out alone with God… we may not even be able to reach out to others for their experience or advice because it's our own path and process.

I remember years ago, when I was a young adult at my original home church (Greater Mt. Calvary Holy Church in Washington DC), a preacher named Dr. Viola Fisher said something that has always stuck with me, and I paraphrase: *"Some of you church mothers are so hard on these young women, as if you have always been sanctified and holy! What took you 20 years to walk out, you want these young women to get and walk out in a year!"* I raise her point to emphasize what the Lord is saying right here: transformational change is not instant; it comes little by little. Although others may want your transformation to occur instantly, it is important for you to recognize that you are changing every day, little by little.

In Psalm 84, David says: *"Blessed are they that dwell in Thy house: they will be still praising thee. Selah. Blessed is the man whose strength is in Thee; in whose heart are the ways of them, who passing through the valley of Baca make it a well; the rain also filleth the pools. They go from strength to strength, every one of them in Zion appeareth before God."*

Here David is speaking of those of the House of God being developed by going from "strength to strength." This speaks of a progressive process of change into a life of victory... little by little.

John Newton (1725–1807) was an English Anglican clergyman and abolitionist. He was also a captain of slave ships and an investor of trade. In 1788, he published a pamphlet called *"Thoughts Upon the African Slave Trade."* He began his writing with an apology for his part in the trade, then he said something powerful--let it marinate: *"I am not what I ought to be, I am not what I want to be, I am not what I hope to be in another world; but still I am not what I once used to be, and by the grace of God I am what I am."* This quote reflects the principle of little by little. Transformational change is a process that you and I must embrace, and we cannot measure our process by another person's process.

Let's now look back and dig a little deeper into Deut. 7:22: *"And the Lord your God will drive out those nations before you little by little;* **you will be unable to destroy them at once,** *lest the beasts of the field become too numerous for you."*

It was during a season of transformational change in the life of

His people that God revealed His little by little principle. They had been delivered from slavery in Egypt, had spent many years in the wilderness, and now were on their way into their promised land.

The nations mentioned here were the giants in the land, whom I call the "-ites" of the Promised Land: the Hittites, Girgashites, Amorites, Canaanites, Perizzites, Hivites, and Jebusites. These seven nations, who were described as greater and mightier than the children of Israel (v. 1), were occupying the land which God had promised to give to His people.

Notice that God said that they would not be able to destroy them all at once. But why did He say that? Isn't this the same God who had delivered them miraculously from Egypt by parting the Red Sea for them to escape? Couldn't He simply cause them to take the promised land in a similar miraculous event?

In Exodus 23:29-30 we find the same scenario recorded in more detail, as well as the little by little principle: *"I will not drive them out from before you in one year, lest the land become desolate and the beasts of the field become too numerous for you. Little by little I will drive them out from before you, until you have increased, and you inherit the land."* (NKJV)

Many Bible translations interpret "until you have increased" as "until you have developed." Don't miss this: growth and development are mentioned *before* inheriting the land. Our painful problem is, just like the children of Israel in the Old Testament and the prodigal son in the New Testament, we want our inheritance before our growth and development.

Here again we see God indicates that the process will take time, by His design. It's here that we glean three key elements of the principle of little by little... the process that He deems essential to our transformational change:

1. **READINESS**
2. **CONSISTENCY**
3. **OBEDIENCE**

Let's take a look at these three key elements that I believe make up the little by little divine principle before I identify the giants you must defeat in order to live a life of victory.

READINESS

When I attended Oral Roberts University for a season in pursuit of a Master's degree in Public Administration, one of the best courses I took was called "Organizational Change." I gained an invaluable understanding of the importance of organizational *readiness* for change. Projects that are meant to change an organization for the better often fail due to lack of readiness within the organization. Years later, I developed an "organizational readiness assessment tool" that all grantee organizations in the subaward process under my oversight and direction had to complete if they wanted to be a part of our 5-year, multimillion-dollar federal contract process.

I know firsthand that without readiness for change, organizations and people will simply not change. Readiness *precedes* change. It is too easy to go back to "business as usual", and lose any ground that has been gained, if this important element of readiness is missing (even though the foundation or old way is still well established). Catch this: "little by little" is the approach for building a solid foundation… one that helps sustain changes needed over time.

Even when applied to business, the principle of little by little helps us understand that people may not be ready for change, even though the vision and the accompanying structures, systems and processes are ready.

Little by little, people need to change their thinking, behavior and their actions. In fact, the Bible speaks of the need for a shift in mindset when it comes to transformation. Romans 12:2 says, *"be ye transformed by the renewing of your mind…"* Transforming and renewing suggest that it's a daily process. Anything that requires a new mindset, by its very nature, will naturally follow the little-by-little principle, because a change in thinking is progressive. If we truly understand this, we will cooperate with the process. But if we do not understand it, we may be inappropriately impatient with the process.

Business and church leaders who understand the little by little principle during transformational change are more likely to constructively handle the natural ups and downs that accompany it. In fact, in my experience, it is often best when issues arise in the beginning. The simple process of analyzing the problems and making the needed adjustments can lead to an understanding of what the organization is facing and clarify some of the mindset shifts needed. Easy victories are not as cherished as those that were difficult and won through hard work. People who tell the stories of hard-won victories (easy ones don't make for good stories) are supportive of the needed changes in thinking. They are, in essence, supporting the little by little principle in action.

When it comes to our personal and spiritual lives, there has to be a readiness to shift from the desire for instant gratification and microwave victories that are not sustainable. Something within our heart should say, "I am ready for change, for transformation, little by little.

Over 50 years ago, the civil rights heroine Fannie Lou Hamer spoke before the 1964 Democratic National Convention in Atlantic City and said these words: "I am sick and tired of being sick and tired!" It is one of the most quoted phrases over the last half century and is an anthem for those who are wholeheartedly _ready_ for change.

In my personal life, there was a point where I got sick and tired of being sick and tired of my failures and shortcomings. I was tired of hurting the ones I loved, losing my spiritual battles, and disappointing my Lord and Savior Jesus Christ! I was ready and knew in my heart, even without being aware of the little by little divine principle, that I was on a long road and journey ahead. I am going to share some of my personal failures and victories throughout this book in hopes that it may help my brothers and sisters who read it and whose hearts are ready for change.

If I was sick of me, I know Yahweh was even more sick of me. I

believe that this is why God said in Leviticus 18:25, *"Even the land itself became polluted and I punished it for its iniquities--the land vomited up its inhabitants."*
God rose up in defense of His plan to redeem mankind, and rid the earth of Satan's effort to prevent it. He took back the land which He created and gave it to His people. However, in order for His plan to work, the children of Israel would have to co-labor with Him, and by faith, would have to fight for it, inch by bloody inch. You and I are no different; we must co-labor and cooperate with God's plan.

CONSISTENCY

Deuteronomy 7:2 says, *"And when the LORD thy God shall deliver them before thee; thou shalt smite them (giants), and utterly destroy them (giants); thou shalt make no covenant with them (giants), nor shew mercy unto them (giants)."* This verse speaks to how consistent the children of Israel had to be in order to obtain victory in the battles with the giants!
Consistency is the nutrient all victorious believers must feast upon. When the Lord says, *"Smite them,"* then do just that. When He says, *"Destroy them,"* do that. When He says, *"Enter into no covenant or agreement with giants and show no mercy to them,"* follow suit!
I have found in ministry in general, and in my ministry specifically with men, that many have made pets out of their giants, their struggles and their issues. They keep feeding their giants and eventually, like a rattlesnake, the giants will end up biting the hand that feeds them. If you are not going to follow the Lord's process and be consistent in your fight against the very thing that is seeking to destroy you, your marriage, your family, your health, and your finances, you will not taste victory.
I have even encountered and engaged with married men who have had a mistress for so many years that they have no thoughts of ever ending it. If you are not consistent in ending the existence

of your giants, you will never be delivered, and your family life and marriage will suffer!

When Jesus says to people, *"Go your way, and sin no more,"* in essence, He was telling them from that day forward they are to be consistent in their walk of freedom from the thing they have been set free from. Apostle Paul would later say it this way: *"Stand fast therefore in the liberty wherewith Christ hath made us free, and be not entangled again with the yoke of bondage"* (Gal 5:1). What we feed will live; what we starve will die. We must consistently eat in order to live, or we will die of starvation. I challenge you to starve your giants and feed your faith! Stop feeding dysfunction, stop feeding drama, stop feeding addiction, stop feeding lust and stop feeding whatever else God is highlighting to you!

OBEDIENCE

Oswald Chambers was an early 20th century Scottish Baptist and Holiness Movement evangelist and teacher, best known for the devotional, *"My Utmost for His Highest."* He shared this thought about obedience and spiritual maturity: *"Spiritual maturity is not reached by the passing of the years, but by obedience to the will of God. Some people mature into an understanding of God's will more quickly than others because they obey more readily; they more readily sacrifice the life of their nature to the will of God."*

As much as we know about the children of Israel, we know that obedience was always a huge struggle for them. If we are honest, it's a huge struggle (and almost a cuss word) for most of us. The truth is that obedience is the outcome of our faith and the means by which spiritual maturity is developed within our life. In our walk of faith (which will continue until this life ends), our choice to either obey or disobey God will either result in life lessons that make us stronger instruments for His use or cause us to flee from His presence.

We often live in the heat of the moment, desiring what will immediately satisfy our needs. What if in that same moment the

Holy Spirit is directing us to pray and wait, or to seek godly counsel through others or the Word? Many times, we even fake obedience by responding with cute phrases like *"I'm praying about it,"* when in fact we already know what God has directed us to do. Our devotion is to swiftly obey Him in every aspect of our lives.

Following and obeying the will of God has made me a better man, a better husband, a better father, a better friend, a better business owner, a better supervisor, a better employee, and a better servant. And it has certainly made me stronger in Him.

Jonah is an example of a man of God who was disobedient and reluctant to bring God's message to Nineveh, the capital of Israel's hated enemy, the Assyrians. Foolishly, he fled from the presence of the Lord. The Lord, however, did not allow him to escape his calling. Jonah accomplished God's will when the city repented, but unfortunately, he failed to understand the nature of God and His mercy. Jonah failed to receive God's life lesson on obedience and in the process, failed to mature spiritually *(Psalm 139:7-10; Jonah 4:3-4)*.

When my marriage was failing, or better yet, when I was failing as a husband, father, man of God, and believer, I had the choice to face my giants or flee from them. Fleeing would mean leaving ABBA, my wife, and my children. Take a moment right here and ask: "Am I running from the presence of the Lord? Is God asking me to respond obediently to His divine purpose for my life? Does God's request appear to be more than I can handle?" Listen for the answer. In the meantime, do you want to know God's will for your life? Begin quickly by obeying the last thing He spoke to you. I know it sounds so simplistic, but it is the key in developing obedience. Obey, grow and live in VICTORY!

Let's jump back to Exodus 23:29-30 (NKJV) where the Lord said, *"I will not drive them out from before you in one year, lest the land become desolate and the beasts of the field become too numerous for you. Little by little I will drive them out from before you, until you have increased, and you inherit the land."* Then if we skip to verse 32, it says that they should not make covenant with the inhabitants.

God is saying to them, "You cannot insist upon driving out what you live in agreement with!" You will either covenant and agree with God, or you will live in covenant and agree with the giants. Here we see God indicate the process will take time because other problems could arise. We also see that their readiness, consistency, and obedience was crucial to His process.

The children of Israel's conquest (invasion and assumption of control) of the Promised Land is a type or 'symbolic template' for pursuing all the promises of God. Whereas their battles occurred mainly in the physical realm, our battles occur in three areas of our life: the body, the soul and the spirit.

Their physical battles were against seven demon-possessed nations, meaning there were seven giants they had to conquer, little by little:

1. The Canaanites
2. The Hittites
3. The Hivites
4. The Perizzites
5. The Girgashites
6. The Amorites
7. The Jebusites

And while in the process of writing this book, the Lord impressed upon my heart to add an 8th giant that we battle daily: the giant of Self.

I believe we all will contend/fight with *most* of these giants, but I cannot say that we will contend/fight with _all_ of them in our lifetime. The important thing is to fight whatever giants are trying to stop you from living a victorious life in Christ! Unfortunately, many of us believers, many pastors and scholars, tend to pay little or no attention to references of the various giants in the Bible, let alone in life. I pray this will change as you continue to read. My purpose for writing this book is:

- To expose the troublesome giants that we all face in our lives.
- To expound on a few of God's proven ways in which He brings forth our deliverance from these giants.
- To embolden believers to fight for a life of victory!

But before we deal with our giants, there is one more thing we need to deal with...**FORGIVENESS!**

Forgiveness is not a quick-fix; it is a process. Forgiveness is also an attitude, a state of mind, and heart reality. And lastly, true forgiveness is a choice. If you cannot check all boxes as it relates to forgiveness, then I question if it's authentic.

- Do you have the right attitude towards forgiving yourself and others?
- Is your mind clear of offense, harboring no ulterior motives?
- Would the Lord confirm your heart is purified of guilt, shame, blame?
- Is your choice to forgive with or without strings?

Forgiving yourself and others is liberating! Let's look at this critical process on our journey to victory...

Chapter 1

The Baggage of Egypt

"Forgiveness means letting go of the hope for a better past."
~Lilly Tomlin, Actress

In 2005, I found myself staring at the possibility of my marriage ending in divorce. I was either going to have to watch it end or commit to the hard work to try to save it and spare my son and youngest daughter from growing up without their father in their life. You see, I knew all too well the pain that my 3 eldest daughters endured growing up apart from me; it's a pain they carried throughout their development. I did not want to impose any more pain on any of my children.

But often our bad behavior tends to remain the same even when it becomes extremely painful… until it hurts so bad that we are forced to do something differently. In my case, the pain was sudden, severe, and impossible to ignore. The warning signs were there all along; how I wish that I had heeded them sooner!

That year, I came to the realization that I was carrying enough painful "baggage" in my life for 4 or 5 people. I had no guarantee my marriage would be saved, that my wife was willing to put the work in with me, or if she would throw in the towel. Aretha and I were in our 6th year of a marriage that had already started rocky and that people spoke words of death over; "It won't last…" was the whispered curse that constantly lingered over us. And all the while, the baggage I carried was dominating my internal world.

Prior to this "crossroads" moment in my life, I certainly had not yet come across the divine principle of "little by little." I had been dragging my baggage with me throughout my life, and certainly was not thinking of fighting any giants. Fast forward to 2018, as I was preparing the sermon the Lord laid on my heart entitled, *"You Must Make Adjustments in the New Season,"* He opened my eyes to see a few stark similarities between my life and the children of Israel. I began to see clear revelations and correlations between the children of Israel living in and leaving Egypt (the place of darkness, the black land, the place of anguish, and the place of oppression), their 40 years of wilderness wanderings, and their ascent and approach to living in Canaan, the land of promise. For me and many other believers, our lives are eerily similar to the lives of the children of Israel: we have our life in Egypt, our life wandering in the wilderness, and our life in pursuit of the promised land.

To those of you reading this book who are fixated on your pursuit of your promised land, but have yet to deal with your issues from Egypt (i.e. your past), I speak prophetically to your heart: If you never settle the "baggage of Egypt," the issues of your past, you are not ready for the fight with giants in the Promised Land. You are neither ready for the fight nor the abundance of milk and honey, because you will remain too busy and burdened trying to carry your Egyptian baggage around in the place of promise and abundance.

The place in between Egypt and the land of promise is called the "wilderness," the place of "wild things," or the place of nothingness. Personally, I call it the place of painful change. And it is my belief that the reason they spent so much time wandering in the place of wild things for so long is because they were carrying baggage that they did not address. They had issues of their past in Egypt that were deeply embedded in their hearts that prohibited them from entering the Land of Promise. In fact, in Numbers chapter 33, we find that the children of Israel had a total of 42 camping stations/stops in the wilderness, the place of wild things. Let that sink in: 42 stops or stations in the wilderness. That is a lot of wandering steps and stops!

They were delivered out of bondage, out of the black land, out of the place of anguish and out of oppression and depression, only to get side-tracked over and over and over, making unnecessary stops, in the place of wild things. They spent 40 years making 42 stops, eating nothing but quail and manna, when they could have been in the land of promise. In the wilderness, the place of wild things, they should have made changes.

How many times have you been at a place in life and have felt if you just invested a week, a month, a year or more in a time, in a place or relationship that was a waste of time, a drain of energy, and a squandering of resources? Your life of victory will never become a reality if you keep wandering and getting sidelined by way stations of distractions.

17

Making the necessary adjustments and appropriate changes in a timely fashion honors the plans and destiny the Lord has assigned to your life. When you look over and examine your life, it will be the times and moments that you made the necessary changes that will give you the most gratification. As the author James Baldwin wrote, *"Not everything that is faced can be changed; but nothing can be changed until it is faced."*

We can actually get stuck in the wilderness of life when we get used to the "cover" or excuse that the wilderness gives us. The wilderness can make us feel like we are moving forward when in fact we are standing still. The wilderness can give us an excuse not to confront our lack of courage and keep us from having to make pivotal decisions by convincing us that we aren't ready yet. The wilderness can even lure us into falling in love with research, fact gathering, and analysis, when in reality these are excuses for inaction. The wilderness can give us a convenient reason not to have to face a moment of decision and the impending rush of change that success or failure might bring.

In the wilderness, the children of Israel could still be considered as "works in progress" not having to take ownership of their new future. The wilderness offers us the same convenient way to delay the change, punt transition a little further down the field, and avoid the seismic changes that the future we prefer might put upon us if it became our present reality.

Deliverance from dark places is such an awesome gift from God that we often take for granted and fail to ascribe worth and value to. We waste so many years, stop at so many unnecessary places, engage and invest in so many people who mean us no good, and completely miss the warning signs to deal with our baggage from Egypt.

In which areas of life do you see warning signs? Or would you rather ignore the warnings you see. Perhaps like me, your marriage needs attention. Possibly, there are valuable and meaningful relationships in your life that unless you change course, they will be headed for disaster. Maybe it's your health where change is needed. Or maybe a defect in your character threatens to derail you. Wherever you see warning signs, don't delay in making a change. It's far easier to prevent damage now than to repair it later.

Exodus 16:1-3 says: *"On the fifteenth day of the second month after their deliverance and departure out of the land of Egypt (in just over a month after the first Passover)...the whole congregation of the children of Israel murmured against Moses and Aaron in the wilderness: And the children of Israel said unto them, Would to God we had died by the hand of the LORD in the land of Egypt, when we sat by the flesh pots, and when we did eat bread to the full; for ye have brought us forth into this wilderness, to kill this whole assembly with hunger."*

In between Egypt and the Promised Land, there needs to be positive change; change that eliminates and erases everything negative about life, your time in Egypt and the past. But when you hear the word ***change,*** what is the first thing you think of? Often when we hear the word change, we associate it with a negative thought or become fearful. Most of us are creatures of habit and routine, and change brings uncertainty and fear of the unknown. Coming out of Egypt did not mean that the Egyptian mindset was left behind. No, in fact the children of Israel carried so much baggage from Egypt into the wilderness that at the first sign of uncomfortableness, they wanted to go back.

What baggage from Egypt are you carrying? What unresolved issue or painful struggle have you suppressed deep inside of you and tried to keep hidden? This baggage is a hindrance to your spiritual life and a life of victory.

I was experiencing the pain, bondage and agony from all my baggage in 2005 when my wife Aretha and I first began to seek marital counseling from a wonderful woman of God, a clinical psychologist named Dr. Deborah Nunnally-Blowe. She, along with her husband Keith, a retired decorated Army Colonel, Aretha and myself all attended the same local church in Odenton, MD. We sought her counseling for several reasons, but mainly because of my extramarital affairs.

At this time of my life, I had been preaching and pastoring for about 25 years. I had brought so much baggage into this marriage. I loved Aretha so much, and I wanted help so badly that I decided to make and keep my appointment with Aretha and Dr. Blowe. As with most men, I had misgivings about counseling because of my hardened background. Counseling was supposed to be for weaklings. I agreed to go and meet with Dr. Blowe but had no expectations that my first session would be life- transforming.

Prior to meeting with Dr. Blowe we had to write and email her our background... things like where we were born, information about our families and upbringing, careers, education, etc. In this exercise, I remember that we were instructed to be honest and transparent, as I am here in this writing. Our first session we had to begin responding to Dr. Blowe's questions and prodding of us regarding what we had written and submitted to her. When it was my turn to talk, I began to share about my background in what would turn into a genuine transformative moment in time.

I began to unpack my Egyptian baggage:

- I was born into **dysfunction** in Philadelphia in 1959 to parents who had monumental marital problems which created an environment of dysfunction.
- I was born into **abuse**. My biological father was brutally abusive to my mother, my 2 brothers, my sister and myself. Each of us experienced our own unique incidents of physical violence at his hand. Today if a parent acted in this type of violent manner towards a child, he/she would be charged with attempted murder and serving many years in prison. I still remember Dr. Blowe cringing in horror at my stories of not only physical, but mental and emotional abuse.
- I was **molested** at a young age.
- I was **abandoned** at age 11 by my mother in Washington, DC to live with a very young pastor, who would marry a year later. They were believers who taught me (along with their young cousin) about Jesus and the Church. (The two

would go on to establish a very powerful and impactful mega church ministry that is International in scope today.)

- I had a **heroin addiction** beginning at age 13.
- Although I lived in a house with believers, I had a street life of c**rime, robberies, shootings, fighting, gambling and multiple juvenile arrests.**
- I was **incarcerated** at age 16 (the youngest inmate at that time) in one of the 1970s most violent and brutal prisons, Lorton Penitentiary, where D.C. convicts served their sentences. I spent 3.5 years of my 5-year sentence in maximum security. After surviving a vicious stabbing that almost took my life, I gave my life to Jesus Christ while being stitched up on a gurney. I finished my sentence and was released at age 21. (My record has been expunged, which means according to Maryland expungement laws, my criminal past has been erased... all to the glory of God!)
- I engaged in **multiple and dangerous marital affairs** throughout my married life.

After all of that honesty, transparency, and unpacking of my Egyptian baggage, my painful past, I still recall to this day Dr. Blowe asking me a ***transformative question*** and then making an empowering, healing statement. She asked me, *"Have you ever received any counseling and therapy for so much trauma?"* My answer was no. She then said, *"Nobody ever got the little boy any help. No one protected the little boy. You needed help and there was no one to get you the help you needed."* I recall her saying, *"I am amazed that you have been as successful and appear to be so adjusted."* There are no words to describe what that moment did to release the genesis of healing in my life.

In a very real sense, for the very first time in my life, I finally felt another human being come close to understanding the pain that I never opened up to share. I was dragging baggage around year after year, relationship after relationship. Aretha did not deserve to have to deal with all of the baggage that I brought into our marriage.

21

However, God gave her the grace, strength and power of love and forgiveness to withstand my failings and extend to me every bit of it.

Men and women carry so much pain, so many struggles and so many unresolved issues with them throughout life, and no one comes to rescue them, no one comes to help them, no one properly addresses the pain, agony, dysfunction, trauma or the bondage. How tragic and sad. I pray that if you are reading this book today that the Holy Spirit will touch your hearing and your heart with the healing you need. Let the words throughout these pages speak life to you and may tidbits of my testimony be a healing balm to you, like Dr. Blowe's words were to me. I am a firm believer and preacher of deliverance. I am also a firm believer that many believers need healing and deliverance prior to fighting lifelong battles with any giants.

The late Bishop Kenneth Moales once preached a sermon in the 90's at Greater Mt. Calvary Holy Church entitled, "If You Face It, God Will Fix it!" He is in the top spot of my personal All-Time Favorite Preachers list… always has, always will. It's because he and I share a strong belief in the power of deliverance.

That was a transforming encounter that set me on my journey towards victory. Make no mistake, although it was life changing and I owe so much to Dr. Blowe for allowing the Holy Spirit to use her giftings in counseling to minister to me in such a way that I would open up, I cannot say that had it been any other clinician that I would have arrived at the same transformation. It is my belief and that of other professionals that I've talked with over the years since my breakthrough sessions with Dr. Blowe, that my collective experiences in the 60's and 70's could be described as me suffering with Post Traumatic Stress Disorder (PTSD) somewhere along the way. I was never officially diagnosed with PTSD; however, that was not a common diagnosis given until the late 70's and 80's to Vietnam veterans. It was certainly not something talked about in black families and communities. Nevertheless, the Lord is a keeper, and has new mercies for me and you every day and for those who are carrying Egyptian baggage and dealing with the issues and struggles that cripple and hinder a life of victory.

That one pivotal session opened my life to the possibilities of transformational change and a life of victory. For me, the work was just beginning; I was not yet prepared for the ensuing fights and battles necessary to possess the land of promise. The transformation of that moment wasn't something that immediately caused me to live a life of deliverance. That may upset some people's theology who are reading in search of immediate results. However, that transformative moment changed my trajectory on the inside. My spiritual and moral compass began to change in that session, little by little.

Please know that I am only sharing portions of my life story here; this book is not my autobiography... that will be written at another time. However, me and my wife's preaching, teaching and ministering throughout the years have always had threads of transparency; that is the only way we know how to share the grace of our heavenly Father and the gospel of Jesus Christ!

Having said that, I must offer a word of caution for married couples: every husband and wife are different, and every couple's journey is different. I know that many couples would not have made it through the challenges that Aretha and I have walked through and come out victorious on the other side. For those of you who are struggling with the baggage that your spouse has brought into your marriage, please seek counseling, pray, and keep the faith! Aretha and I do plan to write a book about our story, as it is a part of the ministry and grace that God has given us. I am a blessed man that on this side of my faults, my mistakes, my sins, my growth, my maturity and my heart to live righteously, the eyes that I get to look into every day, and the journey I walk in life before God is with my "Sugar" Aretha!

Now let's take a look at the more harmful types of things we carry in our own baggage throughout life, into our relationships and significant life events, and into our promised land. Instead of getting rid of the bag, you build your life around your bag of struggles and issues, carrying it into your work, your business affairs, your relationships, and your church. The word "baggage" has symbolic meaning in our culture: it's something you pack things into, and not everyone has the same size of bag because not everyone has the same amount of stuff to put inside of it. Five types:

YOUR PAST

The first bag we could all benefit from is the baggage of the past. Yes, there's value in remembering what's happened so that you can learn from it, but dragging it around with you doesn't serve much purpose. Like it or not, the past is over. What's done is done, and you cannot go back (no matter how much you might want to at times!). Recognizing this — acknowledging the past, learning what you can from it, and letting it go — is one of the best ways to lighten your life's load.

NEGATIVITY

The next load of luggage we need to set down is a negative attitude. For many of us (including me!) negativity feels like safety. Imaging what could go wrong (or noticing what *is* going wrong) can feel like a form of self-protection, a way to cope with (or potentially prevent) bad things in life. But focusing on the negative aspects of life is like lugging around a bag of rocks while trudging up a mountain — all it does is make your journey more difficult. No matter what you're experiencing in life, focusing on the negativity will *always* make the situation worse.

GUILT

Want to lighten your load even more? Then it's time to let go of guilt. The concept of guilt is closely tied with the past, but it's not quite the same. Even if you've done your best to let the past go, you might still cling to guilt, feeling as if you deserve to carry around the blame for something that's happened, even when you know it cannot be undone. Guilt is a waste of time, and what is life, really, but doing what we can to make the most of the time we've been given. Let guilt go, forgive yourself and others.

EXPECTATIONS

Letting go of expectations is essential if you want to carry around less weight. Expectations (both of ourselves and of others) often lead to a lot of stress and strife, and quite frequently you don't even realize how much they weigh you down. They might seem like something beneficial — guidelines that show you what you do and don't want — but they are heavy. It's not until you begin letting them go that you realize how cumbersome they are.

OTHERS' MISTAKES

Finally, something many of us carry around that we really need to set down? Others' mistakes. The past of others might not seem like something you're carrying, but you're likely doing so without realizing it. Whether it's parents, siblings, colleagues, friends, or children, many of us drag around the weight of what others have done (either because we feel partly responsible for it or because we've been hurt by it), and, just as with our own pasts, the pasts of others cannot be undone. Do yourself a favor and set that extra weight down!

Getting rid of one (or all!) of these things is no easy feat, but the effort it takes is so worth it. Life is a tough climb sometimes and lugging around extra weight only makes the ascent more difficult.

In examining the baggage we carry, I strongly suggest you never play the game of comparing and contrasting your baggage with someone else's baggage for any reason. PERIOD (as the young folks say). That may lead you into judging yourself or someone else too harshly. In the parables given in the Sermon on the Mount found in Matthew 7:1-5, Jesus was cautioning His audience from judging others when He referred to being concerned with the mote in your brother's eye but not the beam in your own eye. What is significant here, is the effort an individual makes to remove what is in their own eye.

We know from scripture that the children of Israel carried excess baggage from Egypt because the scriptures reference the "baggage mindset" they carried out of Egypt. This complaining behavior clusters around a number of incidents during the Exodus.

Scripture	Complaint	Motivation
Exodus 5:21	Your demands to Pharaoh have made us a stench to him, demanding bricks withouth supplying straw.	Fear of punishment
Exodus 14:11-12	You brought us to die in the wilderness.	Fear of dying in battle
Exodus 15:24	Grumbling. Water is bitter at Marah. "What shall we drink?"	Fear of dying of thirst
Exodus 16:2, 7-9, 12	Grumbling. "We'll starve to death!" Recalled pots of meat in Egypt.	Fear of dying from starvation
Exodus 17:3	At Rephidim, Moses strikes the rock at God's command.	Fear of dying of thirst

Many of the children of Israel made it seem like life was grand in Egypt, like their past was outstanding. Nostalgia is the art of making the past seem better than it really was. Don't memorialize your past by bringing the excessive baggage with you, for often what is hidden within that memorial bag of the past is the fear of the future… the fear of facing your giants.

Fear of the future is something that we all grapple with if we decide to take a risk to follow the call on our life, make a significant life change, or migrate from one place in life to a new unknown place. It is more common than you think. I've seen many people go through the hardship of leaving behind what is familiar for the dream or pursuit of something new and promising. I have watched them do the hard work of stepping away from what is comfortable. I have walked alongside them (in many of the men's ministries that I have led over the last 20 years) as they have moved into the unknown. I have sat with them at low points and prayed with them when they weren't sure if their journey was going to lead anywhere. I have lamented and cried with people who never thought they would "arrive" at the place they had hoped and dreamed about.

From recovering from marital affairs, long years of pornography addiction, years of alcoholism or drug addiction, I have seen people do all of the work only to get right to the edge of their promised land, and then become too scared to enter it. After all the work, prayer, planning, preparation, hoping, and dreaming, there arises a fear that can often seize people when everything they want is finally right in front of them.

I declare and decree Isaiah 43:18-19 over you, as you let go of your baggage from Egypt and move forward in your walk towards dwelling in the promised land of victory: *"Do not remember the former things, Nor consider the things of old. Behold, I will do a new thing, Now it shall spring forth; Shall you not know it? I will even make a road in the wilderness And rivers in the desert."*

Chapter 2

In War, There Must Be Adversaries

"Discipline in war counts more than fury."
Machiavelli's Art of War (Rule #8)

On March 21, 2003, the US strategy for Operation Iraqi Freedom was unleased on the army and government of Iraqi. It was "A-Day," the beginning of full air combat operations in Gulf War II. As the television cameras were recording, coalition airpower was smashing Saddam Hussein's presidential compound and other government and military sites in and around Baghdad. Reporters everywhere started calling what they were filming and reporting, "shock and awe." That term, which had burst suddenly into public awareness in January, was by March in near universal usage to describe the strategy. In the week the war began, more than 600 news reports around the world referred to "shock and awe," according to a count by the Washington Post.

Military strategists from Sun Tzu's The Art of War, Machiavelli's Art of War to General Carl von Clausewitz's On War, have understood the value of destroying the enemy's will to resist, but "shock and awe," which was introduced by a 1996 study aimed at Pentagon insiders, took it to higher levels. Shock and awe meant an attack so massive and sudden that the enemy would be stunned, confused, overwhelmed, and paralyzed.

When there is war, there has to be adversaries. I have read a lot of spiritual warfare books, articles etc.; however, I have developed my own personal mantra that I have shared in sermons and prophetic exhortations and will now share it with you. It is, *"I must become my adversary's adversary!"* What this suggests is, if I am being attacked with sickness and disease, then I must become an adversary of sickness and disease. If I am being attacked in my finances, then I must become an adversary of debt and lack. I want to become a nightmare to what I am opposing. I don't want to even alert my adversary of how serious I have become in my warfare against it until the time I launch my attack. That's how serious and strategic I have become.

The word *adversary* is from the Latin adjective *adverāsarius* ("turned toward" or "antagonistic toward"), which in turn can be traced back to the verb advertere, meaning "to turn toward; one that contends with, opposes, or resists an enemy or opponent."

The Apostle Peter tells us in 1 Peter 5:8 that we should *"be sober, be vigilant; because your adversary the devil walks about like a roaring lion, seeking whom he may devour."* Therefore, it is not enough to put on the whole armor of God if you are not going to go to war against the devil and the giants he has assigned to seek and destroy you.

As I've stated before, to be victorious in this new season and new pursuit of yours, to be free from the giants that have fought against you, your mindset has to change. Your mindset must be "I must become my adversary's adversary. My adversary is seeking to destroy me, so I must seek out my adversary at every opportunity to destroy them." You have no time to play games with your adversaries, the giants; nor can you afford to ignore them.

Let's look at the Book of Daniel for some insight on the tactics and strategies of the Devil.

"And he shall speak great words against the most High, and shall wear out the saints of the most High, and think to change times and laws: and they shall be given into his hand until a time and times and the dividing of time." Daniel 7:25 KJV

"He shall speak pompous words against the Most High, Shall persecute the saints of the Most High, And shall intend to change times and law. Then the saints shall be given into his hand For a time and times and half a time." Daniel 7:25 NKJV

The Amplified Bible gives us a little more insight:
"And he shall speak words against the Most High [God] and shall wear out the saints of the Most High and think to change the time [of sacred feasts and holy days] and the law; and the saints shall be given into his hand for a time, two times, and half a time [three and one-half years]." Daniel 7:25 (AMP)

Notice in the 3 different versions the words "persecute" and "wear out." The devil's deploying of the giants in your life is to persecute and wear you out. Catch this: many saints are fatigued from a one-sided fight. We have been taking the "hits" and enduring the attacks and are therefore worn out because we are not *fighting back*.

When is the last time you made a conscious effort to war against the giants who have been deployed against you? Do you have any idea of the devil's tactics and strategies (i.e. where the attacks have been coming from and where they will come from next)? *"Lest Satan should get an advantage of us; for we are not ignorant of his devices" (2 Corinthians 2:11)*. If the devil has an advantage in your life right now, what are you prepared to do about it?

Be honest with yourself. Has the devil gained the advantage in your life? If the answer is yes, then I ask again, what are you prepared to do? The last part of 2 Corinthians 2:11 gives us a starting point for reversing his advantage. Paul says we are not ignorant of his devices. Darkness is one of his devices. Too many of us are living in the dark spaces, the shadows of our secret sins, our hypocrisies, our issues, our struggles. He tries to convince us that everything is best kept in the dark, in the shadows; but he is a liar! A great book that I started reading during my transformative season is *"Out of the Shadows"* by Dr. Patrick Carnes. It helped me to strive for the light of Jesus Christ in ways I had never sought before.

Living in the light and being honest is an extremely important issue for the man or woman struggling with sexual sin as I was. Honesty begins with examining one's own heart, thoughts, and actions. In this process, the sincere believer will humble and brace themselves for the unavoidable conclusion when exposed to the light: *"I am not nearly as godly as I imagined myself to be. If I'm ever going to change, I must quit fooling myself and others. I am where I am, spiritually; I'm not on a pedestal, nor in the worst sinners club either."*

Our desire to live in the light has to be stronger than the opinions of people who know our shortcomings. We must ask ourselves the question, *"How much do I care?"* When you get to the place that you are truly sick of the sin in your life, you will be willing to do anything, even making yourself vulnerable to another person. What could stop you? Only the desire to save face, save reputation, and protect self. Real deliverance from sexual sin or any other struggle can never be possible until the heart is opened up and exposed. Glossing over, hiding and masking one's true inner person (the condition of the heart) will only keep oneself locked in darkness.

Keeping an inflated perspective of my spirituality was only hindering any real growth and deliverance. The truth is that I realized that my heart was full of wickedness. My thinking had become increasingly warped. I had hurt God and my family by my actions. I needed to do whatever it would take to change. Being brutally honest with myself was crucial, but that was only the beginning.

In Men's Ministry, I knew a man who had been convicted for attempted rape but was later delivered from severe sexual addiction. He said, *"If you don't want to get rid of the problem, confess it only to God. If you want to get rid of the problem, confess it to another person. And if you really want the problem to remain gone, keep yourself accountable!"* Another man I know who is now living in victory once said, *"I confessed my sin to God for years. I mean I poured my heart out, begging for His forgiveness, but it was within weeks of starting to confess to another brother that I obtained real victory!"* In all of my years of ministry, I have witnessed so many preachers who struggled with issues and yet never wanted to walk the road of honesty, transparency and accountability.

Anyone who is struggling with giants in their life must be honest with themselves and at least one other person. That person should be a godly Christian who is strong in the Word. They should also be the kind of person who is willing to lovingly confront the confessor about their sin as well as encourage them in their growth in righteousness. There is great healing in confession (James 5:16), and it only benefits a person in his commitment to change. Just knowing that there is someone who is aware of your struggles, issues, and secret life and is exhorting you toward victory is a tremendous help. Solomon said, *"He who conceals his transgressions will not prosper, but he who confesses and forsakes them will find compassion" (Proverbs 28:13).* Today is the day you can come out of the darkness and out of the shadows!

Again, satan has many devices; darkness and shadows are only two of them. The 8 giants described in this book will make you even more aware and knowledgeable of the devices that have been hindering you from living victoriously.

1. **The Canaanite Giant** – the giant who humiliates, shames, embarrasses, ruins finances, and devours your sown seed.
2. **The Hittite Giant** – the giant whose name means fear and terror, who brings unrest, destruction, confusion and discouragement.
3. **The Hivite Giant** – the giant of alternative living/lifestyles.
4. **The Perizzite Giant** – the giant of low self-esteem and separation.
5. **The Girgashite Giant** – the giant of backsliding.
6. **The Amorite Giant** - the giant of pride, arrogance, and a sharp, uncontrollable tongue.
7. **The Jebusite Giant** – the giant who bullies, pollutes, and defiles others.
8. **The Self Giant** (I've added this one) – the giant of SELF who makes us become our own worst enemy.

If you are going to live a victorious life in Christ, you are going to have to fight the giants who are confronting and challenging you. With that being said, what will you fight with? I have not written this book to offer recipe theology like "The 10 steps to be a Champion." I realize that many of you reading this book are in the midst of real spiritual warfare in and over your lives, which means you are in fact facing life and death struggles and issues. And I acknowledge that this book is not for everyone.

So, I ask again, knowing you have battled and are yet battling with these giants, what will you fight with? The Apostle Paul gives us some spiritual wisdom and guidance here when he says, *"For the weapons of our warfare are not carnal, but mighty through God to the pulling down of strong holds; Casting down imaginations, and every high thing that exalteth itself against the knowledge of God, and bringing into captivity every thought to the obedience of Christ"* (2 Corinthians 10:4-5). Let's break this passage down...

Our weapons are not carnal – Not those of the flesh. Not weapons as the people of the world use. They are not the weapons that are employed by earthly soldiers or conquerors; nor are they weapons as people in general rely on to be successful. We do not depend on eloquence, or talent, or learning, or wealth, or beauty, or relationship networks or any of the external aids on which the people of this world rely. Our strength is derived from God alone. *"Not by might nor by power, but by My Spirit,' saith the Lord of hosts."* (Zechariah 4:6)

But mighty through God – They are rendered mighty or powerful by the will of God. You must come to the realization and fully depend on Him for the working of your weapons and their efficacy. Paul did not specify the exact weapons on which he relied; but he did give us a clue in 2 Corinthians 6:6-7:

- **purity**
- **knowledge**
- **longsuffering**
- **kindness,**
- **the Holy Spirit**
- **sincere love**
- **the word of truth**
- **the power of God,**
- **the armor of righteousness**
- **in the right hand and the left**

These 10 weapons were furnished by God, and it is important for you to know that they are mighty only through God. Praise is a weapon. Your praise is a weapon. Worship is a weapon. Your worship is a weapon. Prayer is a weapon. Your prayer is a weapon.

Conquerors, soldiers, and earthly warriors go into battle depending on the might of their own arm or the might of the nation they are fighting for, and on the wisdom and skill which plans the battle. Believers should go into warfare knowing that no matter how wisely his or her plans are formed, that the efficacy of all depends on the will and power of God. You and I have no hope of victory but in God. And if God does not stand with us, we are sure of defeat. However, you can be encouraged that the Lord God will show up every day for you and I. Listen to the "weeping prophet" Jeremiah, *"It is of the Lord's mercies that we are not consumed, because his compassions fail not. They are new every morning: great is thy faithfulness." (Lamentations 3:22-23)*

To the pulling down of strongholds – The word rendered here as "strongholds" means properly a fastness, fortress, or strong control. It is used here to denote the various obstacles resembling a fortress which exist, and which is designed to stop believers. All those obstacles are strongly fortified, so in essence, the giants have strong control. The sins of our heart are fortified by how long we have indulged and by the hold which they have on our soul. The wickedness and strong passions of our past failures and sins is the very profile and intelligence the giants have seized to exercise control/strongholds. The controls, grips and entanglements are what must be brought down. Sin, iniquity and transgression used by the giants become strongholds in our lives.

Over 25 years ago, I preached a message "Bent in the Wrong Direction, Broken in the Right Place." Sin, iniquity and transgression, if not righteously dealt with, will harden your life in a particular way, hence you have a bent to lie, cheat, steal and more. The right place to be broken is in the heart. My text was Psalm 32:5, where the psalmist says, "I acknowledged my *sin* to you and did not cover up my *iniquity*. I said, 'I will confess my *transgressions* to the LORD.'" In this one verse, "sin," "iniquity," and "transgression" are all mentioned. I will not go into depth with these three words, but they convey almost the same idea of evil and lawlessness, as defined by God in 1 John 3:4. I suggest you conduct a personal word study, because each word carries a different meaning.

The word *sin* and its cognates are used 786 times in the New International Version of the Bible. Sin means "to miss the mark." It can refer to doing something against God or against a person; doing the opposite of what is right; doing something that will have negative results; and failing to do something you know is right. Our sin nature leads to trespassing. A trespasser is someone who crosses a line or climbs a fence that he should not cross or climb. A trespass may be intentional or unintentional. We all "cross the line" in thought, word, or attitude many times a day; therefore, we should be quick to forgive others who do the same.

Transgression refers to presumptuous sin. To transgress is to choose to intentionally disobey; transgression is willful trespassing. Samson intentionally broke his Nazirite vow by touching a dead lion (Numbers 6:1–5; Judges 14:8–9) and allowing his hair to be cut (Judges 16:17); in doing so, he was committing a transgression. David was referring to this kind of sin when he wrote, *"Blessed is the one whose transgressions are forgiven, whose sins are covered"* (Psalm 32:1). When we knowingly run a stop sign, tell a lie, or blatantly disregard an authority, we are transgressing.

Iniquity is more deeply rooted. Iniquity refers to a premeditated choice; to commit iniquity is to continue without repentance. David's sin with Bathsheba that led to the killing of her husband, Uriah, was iniquity (2 Samuel 11:3–4; 2 Samuel 12:9). Micah 2:1 says, *"Woe to those who plan iniquity, to those who plot evil on their beds! At morning's light they carry it out because it is in their power to do it."* In David's psalm of repentance, he cries out to God, saying, *"Wash away all my iniquity and cleanse me from my sin"* (Psalm 51:2).

God forgives iniquity, as He does any type of sin when we repent (Jeremiah 33:8; Hebrews 8:12). However, iniquity left unchecked leads to a state of willful sin where the fear of God is no longer possible.

Chapter 3

The Canaanite Giant

"Sometimes, life gives you a second chance because, just maybe you were not ready the first time."

Author Unknown

Most people are familiar with the story of the patriarch Noah, who, after the great flood, was spared by God, along with his family, to reestablish civilization upon the earth. The passage goes on to tell us that one night while in a state of drunkenness, Noah was seen naked by his son, Ham, and so he cursed him. Thus, what is known as the "The Curse of Ham" actually fell upon Ham's son, Canaan, whose lineage became known as the Canaanites.

The word Canaan is derived from the Hebrew root kena, which means "to be brought down by a heavy load." By extension this word can also mean "subdue, humble or humiliate." Canaan and his descendants were continually being "brought down." When Canaan was cursed by Noah, his descendants were subdued and conquered by Israel as God had promised in Deuteronomy 9:3: *"Therefore understand today that the Lord your God is He who goes over before you as a consuming fire. He will destroy them and bring them down before you; so you shall drive them out and destroy them quickly, as the Lord has said to you."*

The phrase "bring [them] down" is the Hebrew word *kena* used in the context of the conquest of the Canaanites. God used Israel to "bring down low" (kena) the people who are "brought down low" (kena'an).

The word *kena'an* can also mean a "merchant" as in Hosea 12:7 (verse 8 in the Hebrew Bible) as a merchant is one who carries heavy financial loads. Putting these various concepts together, we find that Canaanite means *"merchants who humiliate."*

Thus, the spiritual giant of Canaanite is a financial giant; it is the giant who humiliates, shames, embarrasses, ruins finances, and devours your sown seed.

I liken the Canaanite giant to an octopus: just like an octopus has 8 tentacles to use, maneuver, capture things, etc, this giant has the ability and proclivity to humiliate, shame and bring us down in numerous ways.

Merchants who humiliate
To win your fight against this giant, you must first become aware

of the three main tactics/devices/weapons that it uses against us: shame, despair, and debt/lack. These three weapons form an unholy trinity in our lives. Solomon teaches us that *"a threefold cord is not quickly broken" (Ecclesiastes 4:12)*, which implies that there is strength in the cord and whatever it has tied-up under its control. So when you face this giant, you need to know that it will be a hard fight; deliverance won't come easy. You will need to *co-operate* with the Holy Spirit to be set free from its tight grip. Let's take a closer look at this giant's tactics...

SHAME – the painful feeling arising from the consciousness of something dishonorable, improper, ridiculous, etc., done by oneself or another.

DESPAIR – the painful feeling of hopelessness; a total loss of hope because of actions by oneself or another, or the collective circumstances.

DEBT/LACK – anything owed or due from one person to another; a liability or obligation to pay or render something to another; state of being under obligation to make payment, and lacking the means to do so.

So when you think of the Canaanite giant, think in terms of its tactics to render you shamed, in despair, in debt and lacking the means to make due. In essence, this giant seeks to enslave us financially.

To be enslaved and bound was never in God's original plan for humanity. Remember what Genesis records of Adam and Eve: *"And they were both naked, the man and his wife, and were not ashamed" (Genesis 2:25)*. Before the fall, they knew no shame. They walked in the Garden of Eden unashamed before the Lord, not hopeless, not owing or lacking anything.

The devil loves to conquer the believer through bad financial decisions. A fight with this giant requires us to battle:

- selfishness
- financial addictions, such like gambling and compulsive shopping
- perversion
- greed

Any of these vices can/will lead to financial ruin, and cause great humiliation, shame, pain, despair, debt, lack, and broken relationships.

It may not be due to our own actions that we find ourselves battling shame, despair and debt/lack. It could be the actions of others such as our parents, siblings, spouse, or children. It could also be something physical, such as a disease; it could be an economic hardship that is no fault of your own. It could be a business partner who commits an act that impacts you; it could be an employee or a boss whose actions are cruel or unethical.

Now I know most of you probably already know who Mephibosheth is, because his name appears 15 times in 13 verses throughout the book of Second Samuel. For those of you who aren't familiar with him or his story, you owe it to yourself to stop now and go read it, as it will help you understand our discussion here. In short, he was a man who as a child was accidentally dropped by his nurse, and as a result, he was lamed and could not walk for the rest of his life. He lived many years without knowing that there was an inheritance of grace and benefits available to him. There are 3 things that God wants to show us through this unusual story of Mephibosheth before we tackle the financial giant/merchant of humiliation:

Mephibosheth was the recipient of grace given through covenant
When David ascended to his kingship, the Bible says that he sought *"someone of the house of Saul, to whom I may show the kindness of God"* (2 Sam 9:3), and Mephibosheth was brought to him, because he was the grandson of Saul and the son of Jonathan,

David's covenant friend. David handed over Saul's inheritance to Mephibosheth and permitted him to live within his palace in Jerusalem. For many years, Mephibosheth lived in shame and lack because of his condition... without his inheritance. But God's grace found him where he was and brought him to where he should be.

How many years passed by before you knew the grace of God? How many years passed before you knew that God has a desire to exchange your shame, despair and debt/lack for something far greater? Can you recall being angry at God for circumstances of life, or angry and ashamed of yourself, or just plain angry at others because you're in a prison of shame, despair and debt/lack?

When I look back over my life, I've had multiples reasons to live in shame, despair, debt and lack. I could have blamed everyone for my circumstances... abuse, abandonment, molestation, a rough life in the streets, and the many years that I went without contact and communication with my blood relatives. I could have even resented my wife's circumstances of having her parents and siblings in her life, but I did not. You see, long ago I learned from Psalm 27, *"When your mother and father forsake you, the Lord will take you up."* Abba, my heavenly Father has been a mother and a father to me all along!

Mephibosheth was the beneficiary of David's faithfulness
Jonathan was long since dead when David sent for Mephibosheth. David was faithful to his word to Jonathan and faithful to his promise. In the same way, me and you are the beneficiaries of God's faithfulness and promises in His Word. God remains faithful, even when we are faithless (2 Timothy 2:13).

Mephibosheth responded by loving his benefactor more than the benefits
Later in the story, Ziba, a loyal servant of Saul, makes false accusations to David against Mephibosheth. Confused, David tells the two of them to divide the land and the money, but Mephibosheth tells David that Ziba can have it all. In a nutshell, Mephibosheth's heart

was to see David on the throne in Jerusalem. He didn't care about himself; he cared only about being like one of his sons.

For those who have been controlled and imprisoned by the Canaanite giant, the merchant of humiliation, here are some takeaways for defeating it:

- Get into God's word more and more;
- Learn and embrace the grace, benefits and faithfulness of God
- Never respond never from a place of shame, humiliation, hopelessness or anger

As you read these encouraging words from the prophet Isaiah, I pray that they serve as encouragement and a lifeline as you are loosed from this giant, in Jesus' name. I believe that these words could have been declared over Mephibosheth back then, and over me and you today: *"To appoint unto them that mourn in Zion, to give unto them beauty for ashes, the oil of joy for mourning, the garment of praise for the spirit of heaviness; that they might be called trees of righteousness, the planting of the Lord, that he might be glorified."* (Isaiah 61:3)

There is one critical lifestyle change that must be embraced in order to defeat this giant: a lifestyle of sanctification. Sanctification must become your reality! You cannot afford to allow any door to open for this giant. You must be sanctified! Your soul must be cleansed and sanctified! Your body must be cleansed and sanctified! Your finances must be cleansed and sanctified! Believers today struggle with walking out a sanctified life, which is a life of separation from the world, because we often want our cake and want to eat it too!

The oldest known use of the proverb, *"You can't have your cake and eat it too"* was in a letter from Thomas, Duke of Norfolk to Thomas Cromwell in 1538. In British English, the last word is often omitted, as in *"You can't have your cake and eat it."* But when the word "too" is included, it means you must make a choice; you simply cannot have it both ways. Literally, if someone wants to retain possession of a cake, he cannot eat it, these two choices are mutually exclusive. Now listen and heed the words of the Apostle John, *"Love not the world, neither the things that are in the world. If any man love the world, the love of the Father is not in him. For all that is in the world, the lust of the flesh, and the lust of the eyes, and the pride of life, is not of the Father, but is of the world. And the world passeth away, and the lust thereof: but he that doeth the will of God abideth forever."* (1 John 2:15-17)

Some very "comfortable" believers almost consider holiness and sanctification as curse words. The words holiness and sanctification have been used interchangeably throughout the years, and I am here only simplifying the difference. Holiness and sanctification both refer to an element that is holy. Holiness refers to the element itself; God is Holy, for holiness is His nature. Sanctification refers to the process of being made holy. A process is taking place to make us holy... more and more like His nature. This process is sanctification. Therefore, to have holiness is to have the element or nature of God who says, *"Be holy for I am holy,"* and to undergo sanctification is to be in the process of being made holy.

Furthermore, sanctification may also denote the practical effect produced, the character and activity, and the resultant state of being sanctified to God (Rom. 6:19, 22). Sanctifying or cleansing yourself spiritually keeps you from becoming defiled and humiliated. The call in every age, and especially our age, is Joshua's call: *"Sanctify yourselves: for tomorrow the Lord will do wonders among you."* (Joshua 3:5)

In the opening words of the Book of Judges, following the death of Joshua, the Israelites asked the Lord which tribe should be first to go to occupy its allotted territory, and the tribe of Judah was identified as the first tribe. Judah means praise. Your praise is a weapon against this giant, and a strategic one at that!

The Psalmist is Psalm 34:1 says, *"I will bless the Lord at all times and His praise shall continually be in my mouth."* When your money is acting funny and your change is acting strange, you feel humiliated by this Canaanite spirit. It will dominate you and cause you to think selfishly, as well as have an unhealthy attitude and mindset towards money. I quote this Psalm because when money is a challenging burden, it's hard to praise, worship and honor God. This giant will use shame and humiliation as weapons to beat you into defeat.

Stewardship in the Bible shows you how to glorify God with your money. Being a faithful steward of your finances is more than managing your money, it's also about protecting the money God has entrusted you with. Facing this giant was a huge thorn in the side of my wife and I. We have taken turns being the main money manager of our finances in our 20 plus years of marriage. We have had seasons of plenty, and seasons of barely making it. There have been years when we've had 6-figure salaries, and years when we've had one meager income and the struggle was beyond real. I remember once, we met with our tax and accountant guy to prepare our taxes. On this particular occasion we had sent all of our documents ahead to him so that he could do his magic. The intention was for us to come to his office, sign the documents and receive some guidance and feedback.

I was stunned when he said to us that we had earned over $200,000 and we owed the IRS a certain amount of money. I kept saying, *"There is no way we earned that much money!"* I am sure I looked like a deer in headlights, and I am certain I must have said to him several times *"Your figures have to be off!"* I would look at Aretha and she would look back at me as if to say, *"Don't look at me!"* The truth is we both were stunned. It wasn't that we weren't paying tithes and giving offerings; we have always been tithers and givers. But this giant, the Canaanite giant, was defeating and devouring our finances, and we were losing this battle. He was humiliating us and shaming us because we couldn't give a good account of where all the money had been spent. I am sure that there are many of you reading this now who know the feeling of being defeated by this giant in one way or another.

For Christians, stewardship is about recognizing where our resources come from and what we should do with them. Understanding and practicing good stewardship is a crucial part of becoming mature followers of Jesus. It helps us develop a more complete picture of our relationship with God our Father and prioritize our finances, values, and lives around the things that matter most.

If we look at biblical examples of stewardship and passages that describe our role as stewards, it becomes clear that we're encouraged to use and think about our resources differently than the rest of the world does. But if we don't live out biblical stewardship, we wind up wasting opportunities to glorify God and advance His kingdom on Earth. I have certainly been guilty of this.

BIBLICAL STEWARDSHIP

Steward is an ancient job title. It describes a person who takes care of, manages or protects something for someone else. There are a wide range of professions, roles, and situations that could be described as stewards or fall under stewardship. You've probably heard someone refer to a flight attendant, who is hired by an airline to take care of its passengers, as a *stewardess*. Financial advisors are stewards of whatever assets you put them in charge of. When you house-sit for someone, you are stewarding their house. If someone asks you to watch their things while they go to the bathroom, that makes you a steward for the next few minutes. Anytime you're responsible for something that belongs to someone else, that's stewardship. The Bible doesn't explicitly say, *"You are a steward of God's resources,"* but this title has always been the way Christians understand our relationship to God and our possessions. The Bible makes it clear that:

- Everything belongs to God
- He entrusts some things to us
- We have a responsibility to manage them wisely on His behalf

Biblical stewardship challenges us to recognize that God is the true owner of everything and that He expects us to manage His resources in a certain way. An example of stewardship is in Genesis 2:15, *"And the LORD God took the man, and put him into the garden of Eden to dress it and to keep it."* Let's unfold each of these points further.

EVERYTHING BELONGS TO GOD

The Bible makes it abundantly clear that as the creator of everything, God owns everything.

> "Who has a claim against me that I must pay? *Everything under heaven belongs to Me."* (Job 41:1, emphasis added)

> Even we belong to Him: *"The earth is the Lord's, and everything in it, the world, and all who live in it."* (Psalm 24:1)

Right now, you are surrounded by things that were made with human hands. You might be reading this on a device that you paid for, but for millennia, God's people have believed that the things we make aren't really ours. The things we buy aren't really ours. They are God's. They were made with His materials using hands He made, and they were purchased with His resources—which He allows us to have and use.

HE ENTRUSTS SOME THINGS TO US

Since God owns everything, all that we have comes from Him; not just our resources either. Wealth, honor, strength, power, and authority belong to Him, too.

> *"Wealth and honor come from you; you are the ruler of all*

things. In your hands are strength and power to exalt and give strength to all." (1 Chronicles 29:12)

This is one of the most challenging aspects of biblical stewardship that Christians have to grasp. There are times when we feel we've earned something by our own merit or effort, but even then, God is the one who deserves the credit and has true ownership.

GOD CARES HOW YOU USE WHAT HE GIVES YOU

When something doesn't belong to us, we use it more carefully. But stewardship goes beyond simply "borrowing" things from God. He's not just loaning us money and other resources. He's *entrusting* them to us. While they're in our possession, we have the choice to use God's resources however we want. We can invest them all in ourselves and use them on things that only matter to us, but God is trusting us to do much more than that. As stewards, our challenge is to use God's resources in ways that advance *His* interests. We need to invest them in kingdom causes and use them to provide for the needs of others.

The Bible is full of passages instructing us to use our resources to care for the poor and those who are in need (1 John 3:17–18, Proverbs 28:27, 1 Timothy 5:8). Stewardship isn't about "giving back" to God. It's about using what He's given us to accomplish things that matter.

Numerous passages provide insight into our role and responsibilities as stewards. Here are a few of the key passages that should shape our understanding of biblical stewardship.

THE PARABLE OF THE TALENTS (MATTHEW 25)

When it comes to stewardship in the Bible, the clearest picture of our relationship to God's resources and His expectations for how we use them comes from Jesus. In the Parable of the Talents, Jesus tells a story about a man who entrusts three servants with bags of gold (or talents) and then goes on a trip. When he returns, two of those servants have doubled the money their master gave them, and he rewards them handsomely. But the third servant hid his gold, so the amount neither increased nor decreased.

Even though none of the gold was spent and it was all returned to him, the master is far from pleased:

> *"You wicked, lazy servant! … You should have put my money on deposit with the bankers, so that when I returned I would have received it back with interest." (Matthew 25:26–27)*

Jesus tells this parable in the context of preparing for His return. It's clear that Jesus is the master, and we are the servants who have been put in charge of His resources while He is gone. It's not good enough to simply not waste what God gives us. We need to ensure that God gets a good return on His investment.

"FOR WHERE YOUR TREASURE IS, THERE YOUR HEART WILL BE ALSO" (MATTHEW 6)

In Matthew 6, Jesus tells us that when we give to the needy and practice righteousness, we can either receive our reward from people or from God (Matthew 6:2–4). But we can't have it both ways (Matthew 6:1). Later on, He says:

> *"Do not store up for yourselves treasures on earth, where moths and vermin destroy, and where thieves break in and steal. But store up for yourselves treasures in heaven, where moths and vermin do not destroy, and where thieves do not break in and steal. For where your treasure is, there your heart will be also." (Matthew 6:19–21)*

We can choose to accumulate wealth and glory for ourselves here on earth, where it will not last, or we can use what God gives us to store up treasure in heaven, where it will last forever. Which type of treasure we pursue and invest in will reveal where our hearts are. Are we prioritizing our lives and our resources around the investments God cares about, or are we reaping our rewards now, on earth? Biblical stewardship encourages us to store up treasure in heaven.

"THERE WAS NOT A NEEDY PERSON AMONG THEM" (ACTS 2 AND 4)

The early Christians didn't simply tithe (as the Old Testament required) or give to the church when they had some extra money each month. They shared *everything* (Acts 2:44) and even sold homes and property to meet the needs of the poor. The church understood that everything in their possession really belonged to God. Pooling their resources together created an opportunity to trust God to provide and reveal his extravagant love to others.

> *"Now the full number of those who believed were of one heart and soul, and no one said that any of the things that belonged to him was his own, but they had everything in common. And with great power the apostles were giving their testimony to the resurrection of the Lord Jesus, and great grace was upon them all. There was not a needy person among them, for as many as were owners of lands or houses sold them and brought the proceeds of what was sold and laid it at the apostles' feet, and it was distributed to each as any had need."* (Acts 4:32–35)

Not a single person in the church was in need. This wasn't because only wealthy, self-sufficient people could be part of this community, but because the early Christians used their resources to meet each other's needs. An American cultural norm that grieves the heart of God is materialism and greed. Although America is the richest country in the history of the world, the average American only gives away 2% of his income, and Christians are only slightly better at about 3.5%. Giving away 10% of income was the norm for pious

Jews and Christians in the first century, such that a person was considered generous only if he gave considerably more than10%. Now, it is considered remarkable if Christians give away just 10%. How has our thinking been so altered that we are so wealthy yet so stingy at the same time? Every Christian must break free from this demonic stronghold and learn to live generously.

The Canaanite giant wants you humiliated and shamed by failures to steward properly all that God has entrusted you with.

Chapter 4

The Hittite Giant

"The brave man is not he who does not feel afraid, but he who conquers that fear."

Nelson Mandela

The Hittite Giant- whose name Hittite, means *terror/FEAR*. Hittites were giants who brought unrest, destruction, confusion and discouragement, and bombards believers with the same today. This giant injects fear and phobias that results in a type of paralysis that causes people to be frozen, broken, bound, and in need of a mighty deliverance from God, which He promises to give. But it helps to understand the difference between a fear and a phobia.

Psychologists often make a distinction between fears and phobias. A **fear** is an emotional response to a real or perceived threat. Fears are common and are often normal—or at least innocuous—reactions to objects or events. For example, many people fear spiders—they experience a mild to moderate anxiety reaction when they see one.

A **phobia** is similar to a fear with one key difference: the *anxiety* experienced is so strong that it interferes with quality of life and/or ability to function. Whereas many people fear spiders, only a small subsection of the population will meet criteria for a spider phobia. For example, people who have a spider phobia often spend considerable time worrying about spiders, spend an inordinate amount of time ensuring they do not come in contact with a spider, and will avoid places and activities in order to avoid spiders.

Phobias come in all shapes and sizes. Because there are an infinite number of objects and situations, the list of specific phobias is quite long. According to the *Diagnostic and Statistical Manual of Mental Disorders, Fifth Edition (DSM)*, specific phobias typically fall within five general categories:

- fears related to animals (spiders, dogs, insects)
- fears related to the natural environment (heights, thunder, darkness)
- fears related to blood, injury, or medical issues (injections, broken bones, falls)
- fears related to specific situations (flying, riding an elevator, driving)
- other (choking, loud noises, drowning)

These categories encompass an infinite number of specific objects and situations; I couldn't believe how many there are. As it relates to phobias, clinicians and researchers make up names for them as the need arises. This is typically done by combining a Greek (or sometimes Latin) prefix that describes the phobia with the *-phobia* suffix.

Kendra Cherry, the author of the "Everything Pyschology Book (2nd Edition) developed a list of "The Top 10 Most Common Phobias":

- **Arachnophobia:** the fear of spiders and other arachnids.
- **Ophidiophobia:** the fear of snakes.
- **Acrophobia:** the fear of heights; impacts more than 6% of people in the US.
- **Aerophobia:** the fear of flying; affects between 10% and 40% of the US.
- **Cynophobia:** the fear of dogs; often associated with specific personal experiences such as being bitten by a dog during childhood.
- **Astraphobia:** the fear of thunder and lightning.
- **Trypanophobia:** the fear of injection; a condition that can sometimes cause people to avoid medical treatments and doctors. Estimates suggest that as many as 20% to 30% of adults are affected by this type of phobia.
- **Social Phobia** (Social Anxiety Disorder): the fear of social situations; these phobias can become so severe and debilitating that people avoid events, places, and people who are likely to trigger an anxiety attack.
- **Agoraphobia:** the fear of being alone in a situation or place where escape may be difficult.
- **Mysophobia:** the fear of germs and dirt; leads people to engage in extreme cleaning, compulsive handwashing, and even avoidance of things or situations perceived as dirty.

2 Timothy 1:7 says, *"For God has not given us a spirit of fear, but of*

power and of love and of a sound mind."

The opening phrase of this verse may explain why Paul dwells so much on concepts such as bravery and spiritual strength, especially when writing to Timothy. It's possible this represented a spiritual weakness which Paul was helping Timothy to overcome. Instead of fear, God gives a spirit or attitude of power and love and self-control.

There are 66 instances in the New Living Translation of the Bible where we are told "don't be afraid." In the King James Version, we are exhorted 44 times to "be not afraid"… let's look at four key verses:

- "…be not afraid of him…" 2 Kings 1:15
- "…be not afraid of them: for the LORD thy God is with thee…" Deuteronomy 20:1
- "…Thus saith the LORD unto you, Be not afraid nor dismayed by reason of this great multitude; for the battle is not yours, but God's." 2 Chronicles 20:15
- "…Be not afraid, only believe." Mark 5:36

These four verses tell us to not be afraid of "him" or "them" but to "only believe." With God on our side, we have no reason to be afraid.

Hebrews 13:6 in the Amplified Bible says: *"So we take comfort and are encouraged and confidently and boldly say, The Lord is my Helper; I will not be seized with alarm [I will not fear or dread or be terrified]. What can man do to me?"* Even though God should only have to tell us something once, sometimes we have to be reminded when we're facing the giant of terror, doubt and fear.

Another interesting fact is that there are 10 times in the Bible where we find the phrase "do not be afraid" followed by "do not be discouraged." Have you ever consider that being afraid and being discouraged are related? After all, the opposite of "discouraged" is "encouraged." And encouraged means to be filled with courage! I have shared with many congregations over the years the circumstances surrounding my giving my life to Jesus Christ, and the infant years of my walk with the Lord. I relate these details because I've seen the spirit of fear up close and personal in ways that not many people have.

The year was 1976; I was beginning my 2nd year of incarceration in Lorton Penitentiary. Me and Oscar Ward (my co-defendant) were in the #2 dormitory at the "Central Facility" (better known as the Hill), which housed 2400 inmates. I was still using heroin and doing "dirt." Oscar and I had stolen some property from 2 guys who also resided in the dorm. At 4am on Christmas Eve, the two guys retaliated against us using Henkel knives, and Oscar and I fought them off as the guys in the dorm began to awaken. To make a very long story short, while laying on a gurney at D.C. General Hospital receiving 24 stitches in my thigh and 10 stitches in my left elbow, I prayed to the Lord saying, "*I give my life to you. I am either going to kill someone and never get out, or I will be killed and never get out.*" I asked Him to watch over and protect me and from that point forward, my life began to change "little by little."

Because Oscar and I refused to identify our attackers (snitching was extremely dangerous in the 70s, especially in a place like that), we were placed in maximum security, better known as the "House of Pain", or "Behind the Wall," which housed 800 of the meanest, most murderous killers from the streets of D.C. We spent 3 and a half years in the House of Pain, and saw murders occur frequently. There was one period of time (almost a year) when the House of Pain averaged a stabbing every day, and a murder every 10 days. My Godmother, Mother Alma Belcher, and her nephew, Daniel Lowery, came to visit me every other week. They both have gone home to glory now, but I will never forget how Mother Belcher poured the Word of God into me during her visits and in the letters she sent. During the last year I was there, Raymond "Cadillac" Smith came back to Lorton. He had been in and out of Lorton and other various federal prisons, and death followed him everywhere he served time. He was the most feared prisoner I had come across in my time there. It has been said that between the streets and all the prisons he served time in, he was responsible for at least 10 murders. Without a doubt, it was the Word of God and Mother's prayers that sustained and strengthened me while serving the remainder of my time behind bars with a Hittite giant.

I encourage every reader that has to fight this giant to spend time in this chapter reading and re-reading every word, looking up every scripture, praying and asking the Holy Spirit to empower you with the courage to overcome any and all fears and phobias! Proverbs 28:1 says, *"The wicked flee when no man pursueth: but the righteous are bold as a lion."*

How can believers become more courageous and less fearful? I would suggest that the answer is two-fold:

- The more you know your God, the more courageous you become. Daniel 11:12 says, *"And such as do wickedly against the covenant shall he corrupt by flatteries: but the people that do know their God shall be strong, and do exploits."*
- The development of your faith. Faith and fear cannot exist together.

Let's go a little further into each of these points.

KNOWING HIM and REACHING A PLACE IN HIM

The more you know the Lord, the more you want to become like Him. In Philippians 3:8-14, Paul said words that have always arrested me and caused me to examine and measure my knowledge and relationship with Him by my love pursuit of Him…

8 "Yea doubtless, and I count all things but loss for the excellency of the knowledge of Christ Jesus my Lord: for whom I have suffered the loss of all things, and do count them but dung, that I may win Christ,

9 And be found in him, not having mine own righteousness,

which is of the law, but that which is through the faith of Christ, the righteousness which is of God by faith:

10 That I may know him, and the power of his resurrection, and the fellowship of his sufferings, being made conformable unto his death;

11 If by any means I might attain unto the resurrection of the dead.

12 Not as though I had already attained, either were already perfect: but I follow after, if that I may apprehend that for which also I am apprehended of Christ Jesus.

13 Brethren, I count not myself to have apprehended: but this one thing I do, forgetting those things which are behind, and reaching forth unto those things which are before,

14 I press toward the mark for the prize of the high calling of God in Christ Jesus."

Paul is dropping some major revelatory nuggets here! The first being that he had a desire to apprehend Christ. The word *apprehend* is a strong word choice that is normally associated with law enforcement. In essence, Paul is saying that Christ arrested him. And if you know Paul's testimony, you know that he was knocked off his beast on the Damascus Road, and it was there that his divine arrest was carried out. Paul paints the picture of wanting Christ as Christ wanted him. Secondly, Paul is saying that *"there is a place in Christ I am pursuing. I'm dropping things that are behind me; they have no meaning for me now because I'm pressing towards the mark, I'm striving to reach the place in Him that I know belongs to me."*

Here's another nugget: when you are in that kind of pursuit, fear cannot tag along. It will not be able to hold you hostage. Take a moment and google the *"In Him"* Scriptures of the Bible." There are so many, such as *"it's in Him that I live, move and have my being"* (Acts 17:28). There are so many preachers and teachers who have compiled and explained these; it's like having health benefits without ever becoming familiar with the benefits. For example, do you have health coverage, vision and dental coverage? Do you know what your deductible or your co-pay is for each plan? If you don't know the answers, that is not good. The same principle applies to the benefits we have "in Him."

Today, many believers do not know what their benefits are in Him. The Psalmist says in Psalms 103: *"Bless the Lord, O my soul: and all that is within me, bless his holy name. Bless the Lord, O my soul,* <u>*and forget not all His benefits*</u>: *Who forgiveth all thine iniquities; who healeth all thy diseases; Who redeemeth thy life from destruction; who crowneth thee with lovingkindness and tender mercies; Who satisfieth thy mouth with good things; so that thy youth is renewed like the eagle's."*

Use the *"In Him"* scriptures as a tool for renewing your mind to the truth that you are seated with Christ in Heavenly places. Personalize these passages. See yourself through your knowing Christ. Meditate on each one until you not only believe them, but you also feel them. While we don't live by feelings, we don't really believe a truth that we don't feel. Use these passages to become convinced of and confident that you know Him, and that you have found the place in Him that is your own personal relationship.

The question is, are you willing to do what it takes to develop your faith? To develop faith, you're going to have to do some uncommon things.

7 WAYS TO DEVELOP YOUR FAITH

1) Receive Jesus as the developer of your faith

> *"Looking away [from all that will distract] to Jesus, Who is the leader and the source of our faith [giving the first incentive for our belief] and is also its Finisher [bringing it to maturity and*

perfection]." (Hebrews 12:2 AMP)

If you want to develop faith, this is where you start: look away from all that will distract you and focus on Jesus. That's what Hezekiah did when he was facing death. The Bible tells us "Hezekiah turned his face toward the wall and prayed unto the Lord" (Isaiah 38:2). Why is this important? He turned away from the world, from people, from his own feelings, from his suffering, and from sympathizing friends and relatives. When he turned to the wall, he could only see God. And he received what he asked!

2) Make the Word of God final authority

> *"My son, give attention to my words; incline your ear to my sayings. Do not let them depart from your eyes; keep them in the midst of your heart; for they are life to those who find them, and health to all their flesh." (Proverbs 4:20-22)*

When you're facing a situation in your health, your finances, a relationship or a work situation, you need to ask yourself one thing: "What does God's Word say about my situation?" Then say, "THAT is THE FINAL WORD!"

3) Continually feed on the Word of God

> *"People do not live by bread alone, but by every word that comes from the mouth of God." Matthew 4:4 (NLT)*

Your physical body was not made to live on one meal per week; neither was your spirit.

4) Meditate on the Word of God

> *"This Book of the Law shall not depart from your mouth, but you shall meditate in it day and night, that you may observe to*

do according to all that is written in it. For then you will make your way prosperous, and then you will have good success." (Joshua 1:8)

You may be wondering what the difference is between feeding on the Word and meditating on the Word is. Feeding on the Word of God is reading and learning what God has said, what God is saying, and what God will say. Meditating is spending time thinking about it over and over, and then applying the Word to your life situations.

5) Act on the Word of God

"But be doers of the word, and not hearers only, deceiving yourselves." (James 1:22)

You know what the Word says; you meditate on it by applying it to your situation, then you act on it by putting your faith on the line. One way we act on the Word is to speak it. Faith grows when God's Word becomes a vital part of our daily speech.

6) Pray in the Spirit

"Building yourselves up on your most holy faith, praying in the Holy Spirit." (Jude 20)

It's really no secret—praying in tongues builds up our faith.

7) Continually give God praise

"Be careful for nothing; but in every thing by prayer and supplication with thanksgiving let your requests be made known unto God." (Philippians 4:6)

Praise and thanksgiving are what we do between the "amen" and "there it is" of our prayer. Praise encourages our faith. Praise is our affirmation of receiving what we have believed. "Praise God! Thank You, Lord! I believe I have it now by faith, in Jesus' Name!"

I close this chapter with this verse: *"There is no fear in love; but perfect love casteth out fear: because fear hath torment. He that feareth is not made perfect in love. God is love!"* (1 John 4:18)

Chapter 5

The Hivite Giant

"Try again; you have millions of alternatives. Fill yourself with the bullets of hope and you will kill failure with one shot."

Israelmore Ayivor, Dream Big: See Your Bigger Picture!

Many alternate philosophies and religions today offer to give their version of an alternative "life." The enemy loves to lure people into lifestyles claiming to be the answer to that person's needs and desires. Lifestyles such as "swinging", "if it feels good- do it", "don't worry what other people think", "look out for number one", and "it's about time you did something just for yourself", can all lure people away from the lifestyle that God requires of them. This is the modus operandi of **the Hivite Giant**—it offers you a "good life" IF you follow its lifestyle, but it ultimately leads you into a lifestyle of carnality and worldliness!

Romans 8:5 warns us: *"For those who live according to the flesh set their minds on the things of the flesh, but those who live according to the Spirit, the things of the Spirit."* God is calling you today to completely overcome the desires of the flesh so that you can have total victory in Christ Jesus!

What lifestyle are we told to live? The answer is found in the letter that Paul wrote to the saints in Galatia. *"For I through the law died to the law that I might live to God. I have been crucified with Christ; it is no longer I who live, but Christ lives in me; and the life which I now live in the flesh I live by faith in the Son of God, who loved me and gave Himself for me. I do not set aside the grace of God; for if righteousness comes through the law, then Christ died in vain."* (Galatians 2:19-21)

Paul is distressed that the Galatians are moving away from the only hope they have for the forgiveness of sins, and hence the expression of astonishment which also serves as a rebuke. The words "so quickly" echo the golden calf incident and the children of Israel in Exodus. They had just been liberated from Egypt, received the law at Mount Sinai, and entered into covenant with the Lord. When Moses ascended the mountain, they fashioned and worshiped the golden calf, turning aside from the Lord. As The Lord said of them, *"They have turned aside quickly out of the way that I commanded them"* (Exodus 32:8). The Galatians seem to be repeating the error of the wilderness generation by departing from the Lord shortly after being delivered.

Sadly, just as the children of Israel and the saints in Galatia turned quickly to alternative lifestyles, the Hivite giant has taken many believers captive to alternative lifestyles. There are many believers today who have lost the battle to this giant. So many believers are:

- Alcoholics
- Dabbling in drugs
- Addicted to pornography
- Sex Addicts
- Financial and tax cheats
- Living in homosexuality or lesbianism
- Living "the down low" (*any* type of discreet relationship/ activity)
- Living with secret sins

And this list can go on. This giant has been victorious far too long over believers. But, my brother and my sister, you can be sure of this: no matter what alternative lifestyle you have chosen outside the will and Word of God—because it does boil down to choice— *"your sin will find you out."* (Numbers 32:23b).

I can never frown upon or turn my back on a brother or sister who has been overtaken in a fault or ensnared in sin because of this giant, because I've been there. While being overcome with lust, pornography, and sex with other women while married, I felt as though there was no one I could talk to, which was not necessarily the case. Just as it was my choice to endulge, it was my choice to ultimately talk to someone and receive help. Therefore, I have and will continue to share my own shortcomings with hopes that my testimony will help someone.

In my 40 years of preaching, I wish I could say I've crossed every "t" and dotted every "i", but that's not my story, and certainly not testimony. There have been times I have disappointed the Lord, my wife, children, friends and churches. It was a painful reality and a hard road for me when I fell. However, *"The steps of a good man are ordered by the Lord: and he delighteth in his way. Though he fall, he shall not be utterly cast down: for the Lord upholdeth him with His hand"* (Psalms 37:23). Notice it does not say you won't be cast down; this verse is saying the Lord will not let your fall take you completely out. There is no denying that we will all face the consequences of our sins.

What I'm about to say I have not revealed to anyone in the manner in which I am going to share it. As shocking as this may sound, I have been considered and offered many senior pastoral positions in churches across the country, even after a great public fall; yet I have turned down every last one of them. I know that I could have been a very successful senior pastor; however, I know I made the right decision.

I was offered the senior pastorate of a church in North Carolina after my fall, and was strongly considering accepting the position, to the point that my best friend and his wife packed up and moved to be a part of the same church! Did you catch that? They actually moved and joined the church I was being offered. For about 6 months, they drove me back and forth almost weekly to North Carolina. But one day, I heard the Holy Spirit speak to me very clearly: "I am not in this plan. If you accept this church, the men who are sincere in helping you gain a fresh start will get credit for your restoration." Let me be very clear: these men of God meant me every bit of good, and had everything set in place for me to succeed, but I chose to yield to what I heard from the Lord.

I took comfort in 1 Corinthians 11:31 where it says, *"For if we would judge ourselves, we should not be judged."* I judged myself not worthy to accept the leadership over God's House. Furthermore, deep in my heart I knew that there were many areas I needed to work on, little by little. And despite my subsequent struggles and falls over the years since then, I maintained my heart's desire to be a better child of God. I purposed in my heart to make amends with my wife and fix our covenant. She became my first ministry. My transformation didn't happen suddenly, rather, little by little. I went to marriage counseling with Aretha; we had many counselors, many sessions, for many years. I also went to individual counseling sessions for myself.

For many months, I drove an hour each way to Maclean Bible Church, one of the largest churches in the DMV, to receive individual counseling. I also brought Aretha along to hear of my progress and to ask any questions of the counselor without restraint. During my sessions there, I was put in touch with what I call a "secret society." It was actually a men's group, called the Lust Recovery Group (LRG), and it was one of the best ministry support groups I have ever encountered. There was an interview process before you were accepted into the group, and you were only allowed to know the men in group by first name only. I was first interviewed by the founder of the group, and then both Aretha and I were interviewed by one of the guys in the group along with his wife. Nothing could be off limits to discuss. I was also required to attend a weekend retreat with a few other new members, along with 3 or 4 veterans from the group. This weekend was filled with discussions about our profile and mistakes, as well as questions about our lives and goals. After the weekend retreat, the LRG contacted me to let me know that I was accepted into the group.

Everyday thereafter, I had to do a check-in with my accountability partner, who would ask and seek to know how I was doing. During this time, we would go over the "LRG 25 Accountability Questions" which were questions about my habits of lust, of infidelity, whether or not I had failed or was tempted to act out, and if so, how I responded, etc. The point of it all was to help me be truthful and honest about every area of my life. At any time, they could and did reach out to Aretha and ask her how she was, and how I was. I remained a member of LRG for close to 2 years. The founder now lives in Russia, and he and I connect whenever he comes back to the states. I was desperate to have a life of victory, and by any means necessary I was going to go hard after it, and the Lord provided the way.

When we choose alternate lifestyles, undercover lifestyles, hypocritical lifestyles, the deliverance and recovery process is for more than just you. I needed to repair, rebuild and restore sacred trust and intimacy within my marriage. That does not happen overnight. It happened one step at a time, little by little.

I also spent good money to attend Every Man's Battle Weekend Retreat - Recovering Sexual Integrity, offered by a national organization founded in 1988 by Steve Arterburn, called New Life Treatment Centers (NLTC). This weekend was spent with several hundred men from all over. They were doctors, lawyers, pastors, businessmen and CEO's of multimillion-dollar businesses. I invested almost $1500 to attend the retreat from Friday through Sunday in Ashburn Virginia, and it was well worth it.

During my time there, I witnessed raw brokenness. For example, the last registrant to attend that weekend was literally admitted the Thursday before the retreat kicked off. The Tuesday of that same week, his wife had caught and confronted him in what had been a long-time affair. She told him she thought she was done with their marriage and demanded that he get help. After giving him the information for the retreat, she told him there was no guarantee she wouldn't file for divorce or be there when he returned home. This particular weekend, I saw men that had crashed and burned, crying like babies knowing the havoc they had wrecked on their marriages. I was one of them; we all had either destroyed marriages, destroyed relationships with children, and destroyed careers. I saw men talk openly and transparently like I had never heard before. At this particular retreat I learned about:

- Masks we wear to keep ourselves from being fully known
- Intimacy aversion
- Brain chemistry of sexual addiction, triggers & boundaries
- Rebuilding trust with your wife
- Forgiveness
- Building blocks of intimacy
- Creating a battle plan

This quickly became a major turning point for me. I realized I was not alone in battling this giant. The men's groups and men's retreats I was used to in the Black church could not compare to what I experienced during these years. I vowed that every men's group I would start from that point forward would be transparent and we would be accountable to one another. I wasn't interested in gathering to talk sports, new homes, new cars, or investments. I desired for men to be able to open up and be honest with themselves in order for complete healing and restoration to take place.

Have you ever watched a boxing match between championship contenders? If not, it truly is a nail-biting experience. From one round to the next, it may seem unclear who the winner may be, but ultimately, the champion is most often the one who was fed the best and trained the hardest. More likely than not, this person will be the strongest and have the most endurance; however, there are exceptions.

Carnality and spirituality are quite like these two boxers, and the one that will win the battle over our lives is the one that we choose to feed the best and train the hardest. The winner will always be the one we give more attention to. Carnality and spirituality are two distinct different ways of life and must be recognized as so. To get a basic understanding of their vast differences, let's consider carnality and spirituality as two types of lifestyles. Carnality solely involves the desire for flesh and physical relationships; while just the opposite is true of spirituality, which is far more concerned with the human spirit or the heart.

The Greek word for carnal is, "sarkinos" and it means "pertaining to the flesh or made of flesh." It is descriptive of a person that is controlled or dominated by his or her bodily appetites. This presents a clear image of carnality. Spirituality, on the other hand, is a Holy Spirit indwelling orientated life and is more concerned with the heart of God and our own hearts.

Proverbs 4:23 says, *"Keep thy heart with all diligence; for out of it are the issues of life."*

The Hivite giant, in my opinion, is creating more damage to the Church, and to believers specifically, more than the other giants because this giant has a strong influence on culture, atmospheres and environment. The appeal and allure of this giant is that "my life or my lifestyle" can and should conform to the lifestyle dictated outside of the lifestyle of faith in Christ. Christ came to give us a specific life, and EVERY APPEAL outside of what Jesus Christ gave his life and blood for, must be rejected.

John 10:10 says, *"The thief cometh not, but for to steal, and to kill, and to destroy: I am come that they might have life, and that they might have it more abundantly."* This thief is satan; but on a more personal level, it's the Hivite giant. This giant is waging warfare against the church to cause believers to seek another lifestyle contrary to that of God. The sad news is, he is succeeding on many fronts. We must always be mindful of Jesus words when He said: *"I am the way, and the truth, and the life; no one comes to the Father, but by Me"* (John 14:6).

Facing this giant requires a different kind of spiritual warfare on a whole different level. *"Repent; or else I will come unto thee quickly, and will fight against them with the sword of my mouth"* (Revelation 2:16).

Carnal believers want to be associated with God while indulging in the sinful things of the world too. Unfortunately, it doesn't work like that. We must all make a choice. Crucify the flesh and live the life of Christ or live the carnal life and be separated from the Lord. For some, that might be a hard decision. If you read Revelation 3:15-16, you'll find Christ expressing His disgust for these types of people. He says that He wishes they were either hot or cold, but because they are lukewarm, He spits them right out of His mouth. In other words, if people are living for Christ (hot), that's wonderful! If they're outright sinners (cold), He can offer them salvation through His shed blood. But because they are hypocrites (lukewarm – i.e. saying they know Him, but not living according to His Word), God said they are like vomit. Wow! That certainly puts it in perspective.

Romans 8:5-7 (NIV) explains it plain and simple: *"Those who live according to the flesh have their minds set on what the flesh desires; but those who live in accordance with the Spirit have their minds set on what the Spirit desires. The mind governed by the flesh is death, but the mind governed by the Spirit is life and peace. The mind governed by the flesh is hostile to God; it does not submit to God's law, nor can it do so. Those who are in the realm of the flesh cannot please God.*"

Today the Church is facing a crisis of morals and holiness. More and more, society has no stomach for spiritual or moral absolutes. Pastors and spiritual leaders who decide to "take a stand" and preach the Gospel in its pure, unadulterated form are derided as irrelevant and intolerant hate-mongers. The public reaction to biblical truth is often so adverse that many pastors are hesitant to take strong positions on issues of morality, even though these truths are clearly stated in the Word of God. Rather than answer difficult moral questions, they are tempted to dodge the questions and skirt around the issues in an attempt to avoid conflict. Preaching and teaching about a lifestyle of holiness is almost like cussing someone out! This same issue plagued the Early Church nearly 2,000 years ago.

Toward the close of the First Century AD, there was a group of spiritual leaders who intentionally "watered down" the message of the Gospel to make it less demanding and more accommodating to other points of view. This was all due to a culture that couldn't stomach the idea of a life of holiness. The problem grew so rampant at the close of the First Century AD that Christ issued a strong rebuke to the people who were spreading this toxic doctrine when He supernaturally appeared to the apostle John. Addressing these erring spiritual leaders, Jesus sternly warned, *"Repent, or else I will come unto thee quickly, and will fight against them with the sword of my mouth"* (Revelation 2:16). The word "fight" in this verse is the Greek word *polemos,* a well-known Greek word that describes *a full-scale battle that is fought until victory is achieved.* This emphatically means that Christ is not willing to surrender His Church to anyone, and He will fight for His Church until it is solidly back in His hands. He refused to stand idly by and let these individuals corrupt His Church. If errant spiritual leaders did not repent of their *active* or *passive* tolerance of this false teaching, Christ would rise up against them with His mighty sword.

Christ's warning to the early Church applies to the Church in all ages, and it is clear to see why His words are especially relevant to believers today. Although there are many God-fearing pastors, preachers, and spiritual leaders in the modern Christian community, a host of spiritual leaders are replicating the grave errors made by errant leaders in the First Century. In pulpits and congregations around the world, truth is being watered down and altered to reflect the inclusive values of a changing culture. In many congregations, pure, sound doctrine has been completely replaced by soft, "feel-good" messages, and the majority of people in the pews are ignorant of even the most elementary tenets of the faith. Bible illiterate believers is what my wife has said for years has dominated the landscape of the church!

Galatians 3:1-2 says, *"O foolish Galatians, who hath bewitched you, that ye should not obey the truth, before whose eyes Jesus Christ hath been evidently set forth, crucified among you? This only would I learn of you, Received ye the Spirit by the works of the law, or by the hearing of faith?"*

The Hivite giant of an alternative lifestyle is different than the Girgashite giant, the giant of backsliding, which we will discuss in Chapter 7. The difference between the two is this: the giant of backsliding takes you back to where you were originally delivered from; the Hivite giant doesn't take you back, but rather, takes you into an alternative lifestyle. For those who are reading this book and know that you have entered a universe of alternative lifestyle living and you desire to be free, I speak deliverance and pray that you will repent in this moment and ask the Lord according to His word in Psalm 51:10-13 *"to create in me a clean heart, O God; and renew a right spirit within me. Cast me not away from thy presence; and take not thy holy spirit from me. Restore unto me the joy of thy salvation; and uphold me with thy free spirit. Then will I teach transgressors thy ways; and sinners shall be converted unto thee."*

There is only one life and lifestyle: *"For I through the law died to the law that I might live to God. I have been crucified with Christ; it is no longer I who live, but Christ lives in me; and the life which I now live in the flesh I live by faith in the Son of God, who loved me and gave Himself for me. I do not set aside the grace of God; for if righteousness comes through the law, then Christ died in vain"* (Galatians 2:19-21).

Chapter 6

The Perizzite Giant

*"It's not who you are that holds you back,
it's who you think you're not."*

Author Unknown

The Perizzite giant, the giant of low self-esteem. Perizzites were people who had been separated and were living in unprotected/unwalled villages. The enemy wants nothing more than to separate us from God and thus our protection.

The Perizzite spirit has caused a lot of harm to so many. This thing called low self–esteem, or insecurity has caused people to warm Church seats Sunday after Sunday with no real spiritual growth and progress in their lives. When you've allowed this spirit to hold you back, you have become comfortable. Your comfort zone has kept you from stretching your faith and venturing out to new things. All is well in your world; you have your achievements and your trophies but now it's time to step out of the boat. Peter _had to_ do it; he was the only one who knew to date how it felt to walk on top of water.

Any time a person suffering from low self-esteem makes a mistake, big or small, they feel like they have just committed a mortal sin. All mistakes are magnified and the guilt and shame make them want to crawl under a rock. Making mistakes becomes a gnawing cycle that also chips away at their already unstable self-esteem. Saying no to someone becomes painful, and many times that they just want to be alone.

"Pioneering self-esteem researcher Morris Rosenberg asserted that nothing is more stressful than lacking the secure anchor of self-esteem," according to Glenn R. Schiraldi, Ph.D., author of _The Self-Esteem Workbook_ and a professor at the University of Maryland School of Public Health.

In my case, this was certainly true. My low self-esteem led to several toxic relationships, extra stress and a sinking mood. And along the way, I just didn't enjoy myself as much as I could have.

Rosenberg's research, Schiraldi, revealed the following signs of low self-esteem:

- Sensitivity to criticism
- Social withdrawal
- Hostility

- Excessive preoccupation with personal problems
- Physical symptoms such as fatigue, insomnia and headaches

"People even put on a false front to impress others," he said.

People with a shaky self-esteem also struggle with self-critical, negative thoughts, said <u>Lisa Firestone,</u> Ph.D, a clinical psychologist and co-author of *Conquer Your Critical Inner Voice*. "These thoughts often criticize and hold them back from going after what they want in life."

There is a difference between being shy and suffering from low self-esteem. As one who's lived with low self-esteem, this giant makes life uncomfortable, even torturous at times. However, change is possible, no matter if the person feels it is worthless or not to exert the effort to change. You see, low self-esteem by all appearances, seems innocuous or not harmful. However, Jesus didn't die to make innocuous people. He died to make you and I more than conquerors. He died to present you and I holy and blameless and above reproach before him.

Those who struggle with this giant of low self-esteem feel immense pressure to conform to the expectations of others and avoid public criticism at all costs. By contrast, Christ tells us not to *"fear those who kill the body but cannot kill the soul"* (Matthew 10:28).

God is calling a lot of people in these last days to do exploits for Him.

Daniel 11:32 says, *"but the people that do know their God shall be strong, and do exploits."*

Let's take a look at a few of the things this Perizzite Giant causes:

- People to be lazy both spiritually and physically.
- People to see themselves as insignificant.
- People to have no vision of a better future in God.
- People to have a grasshopper mentality.
- People to be prisoners in comfort zones.

It is sad to say but the Perizzite Giant has them stuck. However, I decree and declare today that people come out of their comfort zone in Jesus name.

Letting this giant of low self-esteem and insecurity dominate your life causes you not to see any reason to progress or get involved with the work of the kingdom. God will not move until you change your mindset. He needs you to see yourself the way He sees you. Allow the Word of God to renew your mind and cast out this grasshopper spirit. What is your vision? The Bible says in Proverbs 29:18, *"Where there is no vision, The people perish: but he that keepeth the law, happy is he."* People who live with this giant live hopelessly.

Make note of this: The children of Israel's exodus began and ended with water. This revelation is never a highlight in much preaching and teaching on the miracles and deliverances the children of Israel enjoyed. They experienced the crossing of water out of Egypt, the crossing into the Red Sea, and the crossing of the Jordan.

- **The Red Sea is a Type of Salvation ("to be saved out of")**
- **The Jordan River is a Type of Daily Forgiveness for the Believer**

The Red Sea separated Israel from their bondage into their freedom. The Jordan separated them from their wilderness (the place of wild things) to their blessings and their inheritance. The Red Sea represents salvation through faith in Jesus Christ's shed blood. The Jordan represents forgiveness of sins in the daily life of a Christian. The water in both cases, represents the blood of Jesus, which both saves us as sinners and cleanses us as saints.

Man had nothing to do with the parting of the Red Sea. The priests did however have to put the soles of their shoes down into the edge of the water before it moved back. In salvation, we simply believe in the finished work of Jesus. In forgiveness of sins for the believer, we must confess our sins for them to be forgiven. We approach God, no longer as a slave, but as a priest. The water (or forgiveness) backed up a long way, to the city of Adam. Nothing, back to Adam, can stop us from obtaining our inheritance in life when we confess our sins. Confession of sins for the Christian stops Satan from hindering us through demons, sickness or even financial problems. Confession also frees us from generational curses. Nothing back to Adam is left uncovered. Our past ancestor's sins, divorce, mental illness, temper, poverty or cancer no longer have dominion over us. We have a new bloodline, the family of God, in which there are no curses. I am no longer in Adam, but in Christ.

To the people, the rivers seemed like an insurmountable obstacle. But to God, it represented a decisive turning point. For you who are reading, you may be facing what seems like insurmountable odds, but I am here to encourage you that its God's turning point for you.

Courage is what it took to leave Egypt, the only home the Israelites had ever known. It required courage to step away from a familiar and predictable life and step into the wilderness. It took courage to trust God to lead in the midst of a wilderness journey that looked anything but planned. And now that Israel is on the cusp of the promised land, it is not surprising that it will take courage for them to enter it. It is interesting that the exodus story begins and ends with water.

To leave Egypt, the Israelites had to muster up the courage and faith to step into the Red Sea, trusting that God would indeed part it before them and deliver them from the hands of Pharaoh. For some readers, you may never have heard of the legend of Nahshon, Prince of Judah. However, the crossing over the Red Sea may never have begun if it weren't for his willingness to take the first step into the water. The Israelites prayed and the waters did not part; Moses put his staff into the sand as commanded by God and they did not part. It wasn't until someone had the courage to act on his faith in what God had promised and actually step into the waters. God saw that Nashon put his faith into action when everything else indicated that he was putting himself at risk and earned God's blessings for all the Israelites. The risk was high, but it had to be done.

There is an aphorism I have always liked which is a perfect example of the Israelites crossing the sea ahead of the Egyptian army. "Pray as if everything depends on God. Act as if everything depends on you." It is fitting then that the story of the exodus formally concludes with a new generation of Israelites. These Israelites were raised in the wilderness and had not been in their own home for forty years, standing on the banks of the Jordan River, fearful and scared of crossing over it into a land that God had promised their parents. They, too, had a leader. Like Moses leading the people before him (and Nahshon, leader of the tribe of Judah who was willing to take a first step), this time it was Joshua whose faith and courage compelled the Israelites to cross that river.

The prolific legendary worship leader song writer Don Meon wrote the song "Give Thanks." These words, Let the weak say I'm strong, let the poor say I am rich because of what He has done for us!

Let's highlight some weapons we can specifically use to deal with this giant:

OVERCOME HIM WITH WORSHIP

Throughout the bible, God tells His people to worship. He loves it when His people focus on Him, on who He is! The impact of this on us as Christians is astounding! It shifts our perspective from ourselves and our situation to our Holy and amazing God! Plus, the enemy hates it! WIN! I have found that when I am at my absolutely lowest, even when I struggle to form the words to pray or open my Bible to read it, I can always put on worship music and set my eyes on things above. (Colossians 3:2) This always improves my mood, because focusing on the Lord lifts me up!

OVERCOME HIM WITH THE WORD OF GOD

At various times I have had to overcome low self-esteem with what Paul says in 1 Corinthians 6:20. *"For you were bought at a price; therefore glorify God in your body and in your spirit, which are God's."* Each time I was tempted to give in to low self-esteem, I said "No. God bought me at a price. He saw something of worth in me." Having low self-esteem caused inaction. It wasn't true, nor did it serve to glorify God in my body and my spirit, which ultimately belong to God.

OVERCOME HIM WITH GRATITUDE

One of the ways the enemy often attacks is by making us feel discontent. He shows us all the areas where we are unhappy, unsatisfied and fed up. The enemy will use our unhappiness against us. The antidote to this is gratitude. When we shift our focus from all the things that are going wrong and seek to thank God for all of the amazing things that He has blessed us with, we overcome this attack of the enemy! When the kids are fighting, and the food is burnt, and your husband will be home late from work, thank God for the kids, thank God that there is food on the table (burnt or not) and that your husband has a job. I know, this is not easy at all. I totally get that, and it is a very difficult thing to do in the midst of unhappiness. But when you are able to do it, it makes a world of difference!

"By far the best investment you can make is in yourself," Warren Buffett, the world's most prolific investor.

Chapter 7

The Girgashite Giant

"You can blame circumstances, but backsliding always begins in the heart."

A. W. Tozer

The Girgashite giant is the giant of backsliding. The *"Dictionary of Scripture Names"* gives the meaning of the word *"Girgashite"* as one who returns back from a pilgrimage. They were a people whose lives were a revolving door from the temple to the cave, over and over again. W.A. Jones in *"The Proper Names of the Old Testament Expounded"* translates it as "dwellers in clayey soil, or black mud. Known as Clay-Dwellers."

They went from the temple to the cave. From being holy to being worldly.

Have you ever heard the phrase *"from pillar to post"* or *"from post to pillar?"* It is a phrase that comes from the Middle Ages. In the history of Europe, the Middle Ages or Medieval Period lasted from the 5th to the 15th century. It began with the fall of the Western Roman Empire and merged into the Renaissance and the Age of Discovery.

In the Middle Ages, when a person is being punished, the person is first tied to a post and whipped and then moved to the pillory where they are showcased to the crowd for their amusement. Hence the original phrase "from post to pillar". For vivid mind picture, think of the 2000 movie *Gladiator* starring Russell Crowe as Maximus: once he was captured, his captors took him from one arena to another in bondage to entertain the elite with fights against other slaves and even animals.

The Girgashite giant captures you, puts you in spiritual bondage, and has you becoming a church hopper, from one ministry to another ministry and never making meaningful contributions to the Kingdom. This giant has you going in circles, one day you're here, the next you are not. One minute you are attempting to be holy, and the next minute you are "out there" living any kind of way. From one place to another, living haphazardly. There is little purpose in the life of someone who has not defeated this giant.

Some believers struggle more with the giant of backsliding and carnality than other believers. Girgashites battle by degrees. That is, by little compromises. The believer must learn to do battle with

the little compromises that this enemy puts before them. No habit or sin is too great that you and God cannot overcome it. From the beginning with Adam and Eve this battle has been waged.

Hebrews 2:1 in the Message translation says, *"For this reason [that is, because of God's final revelation in His Son Jesus and because of Jesus' superiority to the angels] we must pay much closer attention than ever to the things that we have heard, so that we do not [in any way] drift away from truth."*

Backsliding, also known as falling away or committing apostasy, is a term used within Christianity to describe a process by which an individual who has converted to Christianity reverts to pre-conversion habits and/or lapses or falls into sin, or when a person turns from God to pursue their own desire.

The worst chains are those which are neither felt nor seen by the prisoner. In our mind and in our heart, doublemindedness is what has so many believers bound. Going back and forth, never being able to shake free from the invisible chains of double mindedness! A double-minded believer is someone who is constantly living in a state of compromise. Half of you lives to please God, while the other half lives to go back and enjoy your bad habit. Hence, you are "double-minded."

A 5-ALARM FIRE THAT LETS YOU KNOW YOU ARE DOUBLE-MINDED

1) There are two major influences which fuel your thought life.
A double-minded Christian is always being torn in two directions. They have a relationship with Jesus Christ as their Lord and Savior, but they also have a relationship with a particular sinful obsession. It is a mental obsession and distraction, and it may even have a physical aspect. But it's a miserable way to attempt to live the Christian life.

2) You have a history with both of your major influences.
No Christian becomes double-minded overnight. It takes some

time to develop an unrelenting desire to pursue a particular course. But make no mistake about it, history has a way of repeating itself. Until we part ways with that thing which is "stabbing at Jesus" all the time, we continually find ourselves in a state of inner turmoil.

3) You find yourself compromising your thought life in one primary area.

Satan has been at his craft for many generations, and just as he knew what "triggers" to employ with Adam and Eve, he has discovered a variety of enticements that are intended to lead believers to become double-minded, constantly going back, or back sliding. Satan hates to see believers fully surrendered to the Lord. The devil knows from past experience that when a Christian is fully surrendered, God works even more miracles in the lives of His people.

4) You only experience real peace in your heart when your mind is under God's control.

There is no peace for the believer who is going against his conscience and against the Word of God. You feel out of control. You feel pulled in the direction of your obsession, rather than gently led down the flowing river of God's grace and peace.

Most of us who have known the Lord for a while has come to experience the vast difference between the peace of God and the turmoil of our sinful desires. They truly are in conflict with each other. Gal. 5:16,17 It is a battle that doesn't stop until our soul leaves our body at the point of physical death. At that moment, we will be immediately ushered into heaven.

5) You find yourself giving into old habits very easily.

A double-minded believer finds it next to impossible to stay away from the danger zone. He or she moves quickly in that direction at the slightest impulse. The longer a person refrains from that bad habit, the easier it gets to stay away from it. But the more you "cut corners," the more you find yourself locked into a double-minded quagmire of your own making.

STEADFASTNESS vs. DOUBLE-MINDEDNESS

Do you get tired? Discouraged? Bummed out? Of course. All Christians do sometimes. Here's a verse that helps when you feel overworked and underappreciated:

> *"Therefore, my beloved brethren, be ye steadfast, unmovable, always abounding in the work of the Lord, forasmuch as ye know that your labor is not in vain in the Lord."* (1 Corinthians 15:58)

My beloved brethren. The Apostle Paul addresses us as family-- brothers and sisters. Christians are part of a family that cares deeply for one another. The church is the visible expression of that caring love. And though we sometimes feel alone, we belong to the family of God.

Be ye steadfast, that is, don't always be moving around. Each of my children, at the age of nine or ten, have come down with what my wife and I call "tapping disease." They drum their fingers on the dinner table, swing their feet, tap their feet. Constant motion. They don't settle down. It can drive a parent loony. That's how I explain my own peculiar condition.

"Be steadfast" means "be stable," "be firm." The Greek word alludes to sitting in a chair rather than pacing around—"fixed."

Unmoveable, means "not to be moved from its place." Perhaps people have called you "stubborn." Now you can be stubbornly opposed to God's will and that's a bad place to be. But you can be stubbornly, doggedly devoted to God, so that circumstances and people don't distract you from Him. That's good. Call it persistent, call it faithful.

Always abounding in the work of the Lord. The word translated "abounding" means "exceeding a fixed number or measure," "over-

and-above." Some people do what is expected. Others, out of love, go far beyond that. Their lives pour out and overflow. "Doing what?" you ask...

The work of the Lord is the answer. Work? "Not a good word," you say. "I work five or six days a week. When I get home I just want to rest." That's understandable.

Do you have any loafers at work? You know, people who only do the minimum, and only that if the boss is looking over their shoulder. And who takes up the slack? You and the other conscientious workers.

God's work is the same way. Just a few of the ways we do His work, build His kingdom here on earth, is to teach our children about Jesus at home and at Sunday school. We serve as an usher or choir member on Sundays. We encourage those believers who are down. We make a meal for a family when one of the parents is sick. A church is a caring body. But when loafers don't pull their part of the load, it falls on others to do so.

My sister, my brother, this is a word for you: be "always abounding in the work of the Lord." Always. Over-and-above.

Knowing that your labor is not in vain in the Lord. Some people hate washing dishes because more dirty dishes magically appear overnight. Sweeping and vacuuming are the same way. Things never stay clean. Someone is always tracking dirt on your carpet. Is there no end? You get discouraged. It's only when you consider the alternatives that you get out your Hoover vacuum cleaner and have another go at it.

Your wife may not keep track of how often you change the spark plugs. Your husband has no idea of how often you have to dust. But God keeps track of our faithfulness in His work. He sees us serving Him when no one else sees. And seeing us hanging in there brings joy to his heart. Our Christian service is not done in vain for three reasons:

1. Christ's kingdom is built on your service, stone upon stone. Your act of kindness upon teaching the Junior boys Sunday school class and serving refreshments upon spending time with a grief-stricken believer.
2. Seeing your faithful service brings joy to God's heart.
3. God will reward you for your faithfulness, even when no one else sees. His ledger book gets fresh notations every time you serve Him. In a word, your labor is not in vain in the Lord.

Yes, I get discouraged and I know you do as well, but God keeps bringing us back to this verse to lift us up and help us to see the importance of faithful service. Don't give up. Your labor in Christ is not in vain.

You must understand, backsliding does not happen overnight. It all starts with small compromises! The spirit of small compromises is permeating the church, or the lives of believers. The word compromise can be both positive and negative. For the purposes of this book, I will examine it from the negative side. **Compromise** can also mean to erode or diminish. If you never repair your brakes, you will compromise the safety of the car. If you cheat, you compromise your integrity. So, to look at compromise in conjunction with backsliding, what you have is your inability to move forward in your divine promise land because you compromise a life of holiness and obedience. Another way of looking at compromise is like this:

Putting something = com, **in front of** = the promise. **Compromise.**

When something is in front of your promise, you ultimately will go back to where you came from. To defeat this giant, you must destroy everything that comes in front of you, to stop you from moving ahead in the things of God and the plans of God for your life. You must destroy the compromises in your life in order to walk in deliverance.

2 Corinthians 10:4-6 says, *"For the weapons of our warfare are not carnal, but mighty through God to the pulling down of strong holds; Casting down imaginations, and every high thing that exalteth itself against the knowledge of God, and bringing into captivity every thought to the obedience of Christ; And having in a readiness to revenge all disobedience, when your obedience is fulfilled."*

I close with this. Years ago, in reading one of John Maxwell's books I came across him discussing the word sincere. The word sincere comes from a Latin root meaning, "NO WAX". In the 15th or 16th century in Spain the economy was struggling and some merchant pottery makers were putting wax into some of their products. The merchants that had integrity started hanging signs in their windows "NO WAX." The phrase eventually came to mean anything honest or true.

When you have defeated this giant of backsliding, you can stand as righteous before the father, not in your own righteousness, but in the righteousness of Christ. You can sleep better at night knowing you have been honest and true in your walk not only before the Father, but before all men and women.

Chapter 8

The Amorite Giant

"Pride must die in you, or nothing of heaven can live in you."

Andrew Murray, author of *Humility*

The Amorite giant—the giant of pride, arrogance, and a sharp and uncontrollable tongue. Amorites were people who were prideful, arrogant, boastful in their speech; people who always challenged others and they loved public approval. Prideful people have a battle with their tongue. They reject Spiritual Fathers and Mothers. They always know better than anyone. Bitterness and unforgiveness are the strong ropes they use to attempt to strangle the life out from others.

This giant would love nothing more than to destroy our witness for Christ by tempting us to be selfish, self-centered, and filled with pride. He tries to make us think more highly of ourselves than we should and to be proud of what we do well without thanking God for enabling us to do it. Pride causes critical judgment toward those who can't do what we can do. This causes us to feel superior to them and usually grows into a disdain and disrespect for those we view as, not as good as we are. This will eventually cause us to mistreat them.

The way we treat other people is very important to God, and it possibly says more about our character than anything else. If you are exceptionally intelligent, learn easily, and retain information, or if you are a gifted preacher or public speaker, an amazingly talented singer or musician, or excel at leadership, you must realize that you did not give yourself those abilities. God gave them to you, and they are to be used to glorify Him, not so you can be puffed up with pride.

In Paul's First Letter to the Corinthian believers he says these words, *"For who regards you as superior or what sets you apart as special? What do you have that you did not receive [from another]? And if in fact you received it [from God or someone else], why do you boast as if you had not received it [but had gained it by yourself]?"* (1 Corinthians 4:7).

Any ability we have comes from God, so why do we boast? Simply because the humanity in us wants to feel good; it wants to be above others, to be the best, the greatest of all, or the most important.

We know where pride originated from, Satan, the Devil, Lucifer himself. This spirit of pride is still operating in the earth and this giant is infecting many people with it. Have you ever heard or studied the "I WILL's of PRIDE?" They are found in Isaiah 14:13-14. In this scripture the heart of Satan is exposed.

You said in your heart,

1. "I will ascend to heaven;
2. I will raise my throne above the stars of God;
3. I will sit enthroned on the mount of assembly, on the utmost heights of the sacred mountain.
4. I will ascend above the tops of the clouds;
5. I will make myself like the Most High." – Isaiah 14:13-14 NIV

Lucifer knew he was beautiful, powerful, and smart. His wonderful qualities caused him to become proud. He was no longer content with the gifts God had given him. He wanted more. He wanted a throne that would be higher than all the other angels. Being in God's presence was no longer enough for him. Lucifer wanted to be as great as God!

Five times, Lucifer said "I will" – "I will be lifted up; I will be like the Most High God." Lucifer wanted to rob God of the praise that ONLY God deserves.

Proverbs 6:16-19 says this is how Jehovah feels about pride: *"There are six things that the LORD hates, seven that are an abomination to him: haughty eyes, a lying tongue, and hands that shed innocent blood, a heart that devises wicked plans, feet that make haste to run to evil, a false witness who breathes out lies, and one who sows discord among brothers."*

Recently, Aretha fell so in love with the movie/play Hamilton. She was driving Jonothan, Joelle and I crazy asking us, more like begging us to watch it with her, even begging others to come over to watch it with her. I did watch it with her like a good husband. Only once though. In grade school I studied Hamilton, but while watch that movie/play, I started researching him. Hamilton should be one of our greatest national heroes when you consider his accomplishments in American history:

- George Washington's chief of staff by age 22
- America's first Secretary of the Treasury
- Co-author of The Federalist Papers
- Revolutionary War hero
- Creator of the Coast Guard
- Architect of a system of tax collection to bring revenue to the U.S. Government
- If you pull a 10-dollar bill from your pocket, you will see the face of Alexander Hamilton on the front

Despite displaying the greatest blend of legal, political, and financial knowledge of the founding fathers, Hamilton does not rank among the most heroes of our country's history. Why? Pride. Hamilton's self-importance and inability to take an insult alienated those around him and sabotaged his career. His ego literally killed him. Far too vain to patch up differences with fellow politician, Aaron Burr, Hamilton was shot and killed by Burr in a duel at the age of 49.

It has been said by many people that there are two kinds of pride, both good and bad. "Good pride" is tied to a person's dignity and self-respect. "Bad pride" is the deadly sin of feeling and thinking that you are superior to others and that is conceit and arrogance. If you've ever taken a good look at the word pride, you'll notice the middle letter is "I". When you are full of pride on the inside, it makes you hard to get along with, stubborn, and creates strife and drama with others.

Examining Problems of Pride

1. Pride Stops Us from being a valuable team member.
Prideful people suffer from "Superman Syndrome" and disregard

the benefits of teamwork. Prideful people rely on their own self-centeredness and are unable or unwilling to appreciate the strengths in others.

2. Pride Renders Us Unteachable.

People who are assured they know everything don't bother with personal growth. Their ego convinces them that they have arrived and they quit searching for life's lessons in the people and circumstances around them.

3. Pride Closes Our Mind to Feedback.

Pride deafens us to the advice or warnings of those around us. A humble person is not allergic to seeking feedback. It takes wisdom to understand it, analyze it, and appropriately act on it. If humility is not a part of your character, you will care about only one opinion, your own.

4. Pride Prevents Us from Admitting Mistakes.

Pride won't allow for some people to admit that they have failed at anything. You can fail at something, but that doesn't make you a failure. This giant will cause you to blame mistakes on others, justify them as inevitable, or refuse to acknowledge them altogether.

5. Pride Destroys Relationships.

When we become self-absorbed, we hinder ourselves from the enjoyment of the relationships in our life. Pride causes us not to get excited and celebrate the accomplishments of our family and friends.

How We Can Defeat Our Pride Problem

1. Recognize Your Pride

"If anyone would like to acquire humility, I can, I think, tell him the first step. The first step is to realize that one is proud. And a biggish step, too. At least, nothing whatever can be done before it.

If you think you are not conceited, you are very conceited indeed."
C. S. Lewis

2. Learn to be Transparent
"There is perhaps not one of our natural passions so hard to subdue as pride. Beat it down, stifle it, mortify it as much as one pleases, it is still alive. Even if I could conceive that I had completely overcome it, I should probably be proud of my humility." Benjamin Franklin

3. Express Your Gratitude
"A proud man is seldom a grateful man, for he never thinks he gets as much as he deserves." Henry Ward Beecher

4. Say Your Prayers
"Lord, when I am wrong, make me willing to change, and when I am right, make me easy to live with." Anonymous

5. Practice Serving Others
"The high destiny of the individual is to serve rather than to rule." Albert Einstein

Chapter 9

The Jebusite
Giant

"Words Scar, Rumors Destroy, Bullies Kill"

Author Unknown

The Jebusite giant- the giant who bullies, abuses, oppresses, and pollutes people. Scripture speaks of two areas where people can be defiled: sexually (Gen. 34:5) and religiously (Lev. 18:30; 20:3; Neh. 13:29). The Jebusite spirit seeks to destroy the believer in the areas of defilement and oppression.

The giant of religious abuse and bullying is alive and active in churches here in America. I've been a member or leader in a pretty wide variety of churches and Christian groups over the course of my entire adulthood. This includes "mega-churches", medium-sized churches, denominational churches, non-denominational churches, and small churches.

Additionally, I've been a pretty keen observer of the American church scene over the past forty-five years. This has given me a healthy appreciation for the things that set healthy churches apart from unhealthy - or even abusive church cultures and environments. I started pastoring in my early twenties in 1983 in Columbus, Ohio. Our denomination or organization, Mt. Calvary Holy Churches of America, Inc., had maybe 60 churches at the time in about 20 different states. I had preached in several of them from Boston to North Carolina. I had also been a member of the Pentecostal Assemblies of the World (PAW) for 2 years. Lastly, I've been a member of a couple nondenominational churches. Even more significantly, the Lord favored me with a job that for 5 years, I traveled to 34 states, many large cities and small cities as well as rural areas.

My work had to do with helping churches in a few areas like:

- Substance Abuse Prevention
- HIV/AIDS Prevention
- Prisoner Reentry
- How to successfully obtain federal, state, local and foundation funding.

After that work I was a National Faith Consultant for AARP and traveled to 7 states helping them connect with churches. Often, I would ask the Lord why was I given a platform like this? The easy answer was I was helping many churches who needed education in navigating the funding world. However, in a deeper way, I was able to see things from a higher aerial view, spiritually in a small sense like John the revelator with the 7 Churches of Asia Minor. John was able to see the conditions of the 7 churches and the 7 ages of the churches. In the church of Thyatira there was the Spirit of Jezebel, or abuse from spiritual authority. And in the church of Pergamos the Holy Spirit showed John the place of Satan's seat.

I bring all of that up because in 40 years, yep, I've seen a few things in the church world. Some of them have been mega-inspiring, life-changing, enriching, and transformational. Others have been grievous, confusing, sad, painful, dysfunctional, and even downright ugly. At my core, I am a person of justice. I want to defend my friends and stick up for the underdog. I want to warn others. It's so hard to be still and know He is God in many of these situations. The best thing I can do is give you a list of warning signs of things you should be mindful of when it comes to this giant.

I want to highlight 10 signs of spiritual abuse, so you know you are not alone. And after this list, I will share some brief tips on how to get through it all in a way that honors God, yourself and others.

Signs of Spiritual Bullying/Abuse

1. Spiritually abusive leaders twist the truth to make themselves look better. You end up questioning if you heard them correctly or were misinterpreting something.
2. Spiritually abusive leaders demand respect instead of earning it.
3. Spiritually abusive leaders betray your confidence and share your information with others.
4. Spiritually abusive leaders don't allow themselves to be held accountable or corrected. They bully anyone who disagrees.

5. Spiritually abusive leaders avoid your request for conflict resolution that you initiate on an issue but are quick to confront you on anything that pleases them. If you try to bring up things they are twisting, you are seen as unteachable or blame shifting.
6. Spiritually abusive leaders shame you by bringing up your past failures.
7. Spiritually abusive leaders demand to be served instead of modeling serving others.
8. Spiritually abusive leaders dismiss you when you no longer serve their need.
9. Spiritually abusive leaders gaslight you into thinking you are crazy.
10. Spiritual abusive leaders surround themselves with only people who praise them, fear them or submit to them.

WHAT TO DO IF YOU ARE UNDER SPIRITUAL ABUSE BY THE JEBUSITE GIANT

My wife and I have given counsel on a number of occasions to those who have been seeking our counsel, so much so it would fill a book. But here are a few brief things I would like to say to the those who are facing this giant of religious abuse. I truly believe that love will win and spiritually abusive leaders will ALWAYS be exposed, eventually. Ask God. In some instances, it's clear that you need to leave. In cases of sexual abuse, you need to go to the authorities. I have heard of way too many cases where criminal activity was covered up by churches and you need to know it's ok to leave. Other than that, you need to make sure you are following the right way to confront an issue according to Matthew 18. Let God show you what He sees. Find out what is your responsibility and what isn't. Please do not cause yourself pain and suffering with God for seeking revenge, attacking leaders, for the scripture says, "touch not my anointed and do my prophets no harm."

Seek wise counsel. If you're on staff at a church it can be much more complicated, so seek wise counsel. Even with spiritual abuse, there is a right way to handle it and a wrong way. You want to be sure you are in a good place in your heart so you can approach even the spiritually abusive person in love. I'd offer one word of warning … depending on what level of abuse it is … they may not be safe to confront alone or at all.

Move on well. If you choose to leave the situation or church remember those who don't believe you who are still supporting the abusive person aren't those you are called to walk with anyway. End well by not gossiping or sharing your pain with those who may stay. It will only bring more division to the body. Give people who don't understand what you went through, the grace to be where God's called them to be.

Find your inner peace. The truth always comes out. Guard your mind and don't let it take up space anymore. Guard your words and speak the truth with humility, grace, and mercy. Give God every reason to defend you. Think upon things that are lovely and good (Phil 4). You will become what you think about so use your thoughts wisely. Don't let bitterness take over. Forgive and find peace.

Pray for them. Remember it may not be known to the masses yet because God is still giving them time to repent. Be like Stephen and pray for those who are stoning you – they may end up converting like Saul who became the awesome Apostle Paul. And at some point – it's ok to not pray for them at all. There is no need to stay emotionally tied to a place God released you from.

Don't feel bad. Be prepared that they may not repent or change … and if they are exposed … it's not your fault. Their choices put them in that position. Not you. Even if you feel like you should've done more, remember God wants you to manage you. He isn't in a pickle because you weren't strong enough to stand up to the abuse. When it comes as a surprise … no one is strong enough.

If you think you are under spiritually abusive authority, find someone experienced to talk to. Often times confronting that person will not make it better right away and you need a strategy. You need to decide if it's worth confronting or not. If you confront them, you need to be prepared for their response. If you decide to walk away, you still need to be prepared for their response. Having someone help you walk through it will benefit you in more ways than you can imagine right now.

Don't Put Up with Religious Abuse. There is much more to say on this topic. However, the bottom line is that it is not God's will for His people to be humiliated, shamed, denigrated, or violated by those who claim to have spiritual authority and a leadership call. If you, or someone you know, is in a situation on the lower end of the scale it may be possible to bring correction and improvement. If, however, you are in an abusive, somewhat isolated, or deeply dysfunctional faith community that is not accountable, you should seek to escape it as soon as possible. Recovery from spiritual abuse is not instant or easy but it is possible. May grace guide you, or a person or persons for whom you care, into freedom from religious abuse and bullying as you reach for the true and wondrous wholeness and abundant life we are given in Jesus Christ.

Chapter 10

The Self–Destructive Giant

**When the Giant Slayer
Becomes the Giant that Needs to be Slayed**

*"The greatest way to defeat your enemy is to not
become your enemy."*

Marcus Aurelius

The Self-Destructive Giant. Many of us have experienced becoming our own worst enemy. We wonder how it happened. Often, we can figure out how, or at least understand how others have done so. Sometimes, we can't or don't figure out how it happened at our own hands. Sometimes we can predict that other people are very likely to become their own enemies. We see them going down paths leading eventually to destruction or abandonment of their own goals. We want to warn them, but warnings are only sometimes heeded but are often ignored. However, looking in the mirror and seeing our real self, flaws, mistakes, attitudes, behaviors, etc., that can be hard, painful and crushing.

"Man in the Mirror" is a song recorded by Michael Jackson, with lyrics and music by Glen Ballard and Siedah Garrett, and produced by Jackson and Quincy Jones. It was released on February 6, 1988 as the fourth single from his seventh solo album, Bad. The year was 1988, and the world was in the enthralling season of Michael Jackson and his astounding album Thriller. Featuring "Billie Jean" and other classics produced by Quincy Jones, it's the astounding apex of Michael-mania, as few then could remain indifferent to this soul phenomenon. Michael seemed to be a miracle, all the things he was, the songs, singing, and of course, the dancing, crystallized by the magic moonwalk. We couldn't get enough of it. Not only were multitudes entranced and enraptured by the pure passion he injected into anything he did, we were all waking up to the realization that Michael was more than a remarkable entertainer – one of the great song & dance men in the history of American music and show-biz – had become a seriously great songwriter.

News started to spread in 1985 to 1986 that he was working on the follow-up to Thriller, again to be produced by Quincy. What was surprising is that Quincy Jones said for the first time ever, Michael was going to adopt a song written from an outsider. The Man in the Mirror, was written by a great up and coming singer and songwriter named Siedah Garrett. Siedah has said on many occasions that Quincy opening the door to work with Michael changed her entire life and that if she never wanted to work a day the rest of her life, Man In the Mirror has set her and her family for a lifetime. Siedah Garrett has also stated that she has not only sang the song throughout the world, but that from around the world she has received countless responses from people that this song had a great influence on them changing their ways.

Becoming our own worst enemies is a gradual process. The nightmare scenarios and circumstances we create for ourselves often develop over a period of years or decades. The process is insidious, like a disease with symptoms that are at first ambiguous, easily mistaken for or confused with normal processes. I recall a preacher describe a spiritual warfare sermon preached by a prophetic preacher, and he described one of Satan's biggest strategies for destroying people's lives is to poke holes in the souls during their childhood. The soul is where our mind, will and emotions reside. The preacher said the holes are poked by cruel and mean words spoken to the child, holes are poked through the abuse, cruelty and neglect children experience often times by the very caretakers they should feel safe with. He went on to say by the time they were 18, their self-esteem and worth would be shattered or completely nonexistent. When I heard this description of this spiritual warfare message, never got the name of the preacher, but from that time on, I kept thinking of myself and probably the millions of people who as children had holes poked into their souls.

I thought of ten areas where Satan pokes holes into the souls of humanity, our mind, will and emotions, our sense of security, our values and attitudes, our beliefs, our choices, our sense of love and desires, and our spiritual needs.

I thought about the many men and women who have fallen from grace. (Shut that judgmental spirit down now). The prophet Isaiah says, *"All we like sheep have gone astray; we have turned every one to his own way; and the LORD hath laid on him the iniquity of us all"* (Isaiah 53:6). The last time I checked, ALL means ALL, at the exclusion of NONE! So, as I was saying, in 43 years of salvation and 40 years of preaching, I've seen more than my share of believers from Bishops, Pastors, Teachers, Apostles, Prophets, Musicians,

Ushers and Greeters, go astray. I have been chief among them. The issue often times for some is whether their fall was private or public. I can say here that the church, the Body of Christ has failed miserably in how we address both public and private failings. That is why I want to look at the giant slayer of giant slayers, who also became a giant that needed to slay the giant of self-our beloved David.

David and his failing with Bathsheba is a great example. David is the superstar example of a giant slayer in the Bible. We all would be hard pressed to find a giant slayer equal to David. Furthermore, David's multiple sins with Bathsheba demonstrates how he became a Giant that needed to be slayed. The adultery, the conspiracy to commit murder, the harm he caused in the ranks of his soldiers and military command structure, etc., he became a giant in the life of others. For David, and for you and I, our sins and short comings often can be traced to the violation of boundaries.

Let's look at David's violations of boundaries. There were many! Let's start with 1 Samuel 11:1: *"And it came to pass, after the year was expired, at the time when kings go forth to battle, that David sent Joab, and his servants with him, and all Israel; and they destroyed the children of Ammon, and besieged Rabbah. But David tarried still at Jerusalem."* We see in this verse that at the time of spring David sent forth his army and a great victory occurs. But David did not go with the army as he customarily would have.

Spring was the time when kings went to war because the weather was warmer and easier for the men to camp without difficulty. Also, the rain or in a few cases, snow had eased up and the paths would open, and you could use chariots with horses and not be stuck in the mud. Thirdly, it was the time of the wheat and barley harvest. An invading army could live off of the food from the harvest as it moved across the landscape conquering.

In the natural for us, at the writing of this book spring has passed. But nevertheless, in the spiritual, we are in a season of war. To ignore the war, not engage as we should, or minimize it will take us out of position.

Genesis 49:8 states that when Jacob was at the end of his life he spoke prophetically over all of his sons, and when he called Judah, which means PRAISE, Jacob prophesied, "Judah, your brothers will praise you; your hand will be on the neck of your enemies; and your father's sons will bow down to you. Your praise, my praise are weapons, and David represents Judah. Judah also always went first.

- As the sons of Israel broke camp, Judah led the way (Num.2:9).
- When Israel went to war, Judah was first to battle (Judges 1:1-2, 20:18).
- The tribe of Judah always camped to the east of the Tent of Meeting, strategically positioned before the only entrance into the Tabernacle (Num. 2:3).
- Jesus came from the tribe of Judah.

David was supposed to go to war at the proper time, but he did not. Maybe he felt his reign was secure and he did not need to go. Perhaps he was tired from the past season of war. Whatever the reason was, David was out of position. This proved to be very dangerous for him. You all know the story, as he stayed home, he was on his rooftop at night, saw Bathsheba and the rest is history. An epic failure ensued for King David. In his epic failure, this giant slayer violated the boundary of:

- His leadership- he was not leading but rather behind the men at home
- His covenant relationship was broken
- His marital fidelity was broken
- He broke the fidelity of another couple
- He had a loyal captain in his army positioned to be murdered

Some do not want to admit this, but seasons of warfare are unavoidable. Battle, warfare and fighting are inherently spiritual terms from God's perspective, and necessary for us to understand. We don't fight or war as the world does, but nonetheless we are engaged in a very real spiritual conflict. How we war determines the results of our engagement. When we behave as though the battle isn't real, we make ourselves vulnerable to attack and defeat. The Judah anointing is the key for us to win the battle ahead. If Judah stays behind and does not lead, even as David did, something else will begin to occupy the land God has called us to claim for our inheritance.

I've referenced this passage in 2 Corinthians 10:4-5 a couple times in this book because it needs to be emphasized. It reads, *"For the weapons of our warfare are not carnal but mighty in God for pulling down strongholds, casting down arguments and every high thing that exalts itself against the knowledge of God, bringing every thought into captivity to the obedience of Christ..."*

There are some cruel giants, some painful issues and some nasty strongholds that need to be brought down in our time and especially in this season. Unleash the weapon of your praise and let Judah begin to conquer ground. Open your mouth and praise the Lord! As you do, you will be in position, engaged in the battle and not on the sidelines open for deception, temptation and attack. Whatever you are facing, there is a path to victory. Judah is our sword to forge a new path through all the warfare of the second heaven. We will rule in the midst of our enemies! We will praise the Lord while we even have one breath! Take some time, right now, wherever you are to **let Judah out. You won't be disappointed you did!** David suffered consequences for his epic failing, there is no denying that, but out of it, he found his way back to the Lord, and God was able to use him in many and mighty ways. His cry, has been my cry at points in my life, recovering from spiritual and moral shortcomings. He said in one of the powerful verses of scripture, ***"Create in me a clean heart,*** *O God; and **renew** a **right spirit** within **me**. Cast **me** not away from thy presence; and take not thy holy spirit from me. Restore unto **me** the joy of thy salvation; and uphold **me** with thy free **spirit**. Then will I teach*

transgressors thy ways; and sinners shall be converted unto thee"
(Psalm 51:10).

Remember that boundaries work in two (2) directions, it keeps
you protected from getting out of order or position, or falling, but
it also protects you from what could be coming to take you out.
Healthy emotional and relational boundaries are key to having
successful relationships and dealing with life well. The following
Ten (10) Laws of Boundaries are from the book, Boundaries: When
To Say Yes, How To Say No, To Take Control of Your Life, by Dr.
Henry Cloud and Dr. John Townsend, one of the many resources
that helped me on my path for victory. It provides principles for
learning and applying healthy boundaries.

1. **The Law of Sowing and Reaping**
   Our actions have consequences and rewards.
2. **The Law of Responsibility**
   We are responsible to each other, but not for each other.
3. **The Law of Power**
   We have power over some things; we don't have power over
   others (including changing people).
4. **The Law of Respect**
   If we wish for others to respect our boundaries, we need to
   respect theirs.
5. **The Law of Motivation**
   We must be free to say no before we can whole-heartedly say
   yes.
6. **The Law of Evaluation**
   We need to evaluate the pain our boundaries cause others.
7. **The Law of Proactivity**
   We take action to solve problems based on our values, wants,
   and needs.
8. **The Law of Envy**
   We will never get what we want if we focus outside our
   boundaries onto what others have.

9. **The Law of Activity**

We need to take the initiative in setting limits rather than be passive.

10. **The Law of Exposure**

We need to communicate our boundaries to each other.

Chapter 11

CONCLUSION

9 ACTION ITEMS FOR DEFEATING YOUR GIANTS

"Fight the good fight of faith…"
1 Timothy 6:12

God wants each one of us to possess everything He has for us. He wants to teach us how to fight the good fight of faith using His Word.

One thing that is critical for victory in any fight, whether it be a street fight, a professional fight, or the theater of war, is having a DEFENSE. This is so important because your victory or defeat hinges on how good your defense is!

Most experts rate the top 10 defensive boxers in terms of their level of defensive skill without weight class distinction. These boxers are on most boxers lists of top 10 Defensive Style Boxing Champions!

1. Willie Pep (Lightweight) Pep's career spanned 26 years while tallying an unprecedented 241 bouts with only 11 losses.
2. Pernell "Sweet Pea" Whitaker (Lightweight)
3. Wilfred Benitez (Welterweight)
4. Floyd Mayweather Jr. (Junior Lightweight)
5. Henry Armstrong (Welterweight)
6. Ronald "Winky" Wright (Junior Middleweight)
7. Bernard Hopkins (Middleweight)
8. James Toney (Middleweight)
9. Roy Jones Jr. (Middleweight)
10. Juan Manuel Marquez (Featherweight)

No matter how good you are offensively as a fighter, sooner or later you will come up against someone or something that has more offensive firepower than you. It doesn't mean that because their offensive fire power is stronger than yours, that you will automatically lose. What will you do when you are under attack from an enemy, an attacker, a giant who not only has more firepower than you, but is hell bent on defeating you, destroying you? You will need a strategy. Here are 9 Strategic Action Items you need to incorporate in your overall spiritual warfare plan.

Action Item #1 – Always Bring Faith to the Fight. *"Be sober, be vigilant, because your adversary the devil walketh about as a roaring lion, seeking whom he may devour."* (1 Peter 5:8)

W.E. Vines dictionary says the Greek meaning of the word "devour" means "to eat up." Therefore, you need to realize that the Giants, the spiritual forces set against your life want to eat up your growth, your abundance and your fruitfulness. So, you need to be prepared!

Ephesians 6:12-18 says, *"For we wrestle not against flesh and blood, but against principalities, against powers, against the rulers of the darkness of this world, against spiritual wickedness in high places. Wherefore take unto you the whole armour of God, that ye may be able to withstand in the evil day, and having done all, to stand. Stand therefore, having your loins girt about with truth, and having on the breastplate of righteousness; And your feet shod with the preparation of the gospel of peace; Above all, taking the shield of faith, wherewith ye shall be able to quench all the fiery darts of the wicked. And take the helmet of salvation, and the sword of the Spirit, which is the word of God: Praying always with all prayer and supplication in the Spirit, and watching thereunto with all perseverance and supplication for all saints."*

Let's focus in on verse 16. Paul says something that I truly believe goes in one ear and out the other for some. *"Above all, taking the shield of faith, wherewith ye shall be able to quench all the fiery darts of the wicked one."* There is great emphasis on putting on all the armor God supplies, and yet Paul says, *"above all, taking the shield of faith."* He is saying make sure you always have your shield of faith during your battles because there will come a time you will need to stop some attacks and yes, there will be times when you must counter attack. You must not ever go into battle without bringing faith to the fight. We are so quick to use faith as an ATM card to get, get, get but Paul gives us a critical application of faith, it can put a stop to some stuff. I personally know the power of faith as a shield and a weapon. When your faith is an active faith, you see the Lord manifesting the impossible in your life.

The Passion Translation says it this way, *"Because of this, you must wear all the armor that God provides so you're protected as you confront the slanderer, for you are destined for all things and will rise victorious. Put on truth as a belt to strengthen you to stand in triumph. Put on holiness as the protective armor that covers your heart. Stand on your feet alert, then you'll always be ready to share the blessings of peace. In every battle, take faith as your wrap-around shield, for it is able to extinguish the blazing arrows coming at you from the Evil One. Embrace the power of salvation's full deliverance, like a helmet to protect your thoughts from lies. And take the mighty razor-sharp Spirit-sword of the spoken Word of God. In every battle take faith above all else."*

Action Item #2 – Pray every morning. Start your day every morning with prayer as part of a plan to build a wall of protection around your life. In Psalm 5:3, David wrote of his commitment to spend time with God every morning. He said, *"My voice shalt thou hear in the morning, O Lord; in the morning will I direct my prayer unto thee, and will look up."*

Notice the last part of that verse says "and will look up." David knew he needed to "look up" every morning — and so do you. David was surrounded by enemies, both inside and outside his home, and he was tempted to struggle emotionally as a result. He knew he needed to start every day by "looking up" or things would escalate to a point that could take him down.

Likewise, *you* need to start every day with the Lord by "looking up" — or life will quickly take you down. If you neglect "looking up," you'll end up troubled, nervous, worried, and you will lack spiritual power in your life. But if you practice "looking up," you'll be at peace. You will feel confident that you've done what is right, and you'll experience power to overcome the daily problems you face in life.

Ephesians 6:18 says, "Praying *always*..." You may ask, "Is that really possible?" Yes, it is. You can actually learn to live in a *continual* state of fellowshipping with the Lord in prayer. Becoming intentional about beginning each day with prayer confirms your commitment to God that you are serious. It opens your heart to receive from Him, and it sets the tone for your day as you expect God's guiding presence and His goodness to manifest in your life.

As you set your heart to begin each day in prayer — and to stay in a prayerful mindset the whole day — you'll find yourself becoming more spiritually attuned to the things around you. Prayer will heighten your spiritual sensitivity — and you need that in these last days!

Action Item #3 - Read the Bible every day. Make a commitment to read the Bible every day as part of a plan to build a wall of protection around your life. In Psalm 119:105, David said: *"Thy word is a lamp unto my feet, and a light unto my path."* You must make the commitment that the Word of God will be the guiding light that leads you down every path and in every decision you make in life.

God told Joshua, *"... Turn not from it to the right hand or to the left, that thou mayest prosper whithersoever thou goest"* (Joshua 1:7). According to this verse, a great part of your daily victory depends on you faithfully sticking with the Word of God and not allowing other voices or other ideas to sidetrack you along the way.

By taking time to read the Bible and allowing its words to enter into your heart and mind, you will give God the ability to do a supernatural work in your heart and to keep your soul free from the enemy's entrapments.

If you don't know where to start reading, find a Bible-reading plan to help keep you on track as a system of personal accountability. The Bible will feed you, help you, keep you on track in life, and keep your heart soft before the Lord.

I exhort you to make God's Word the highest priority of your life — to put it into your eyes every morning. Let it fill your eyes, flood your mind, touch your heart, and become your guide. Your life will be strengthened and changed if you will do this.

Hebrews 4:12 says, *"For the word of God is quick, and powerful, and sharper than any two-edged sword, piercing even to the dividing asunder of soul and spirit, and of the joints and marrow, and is a discerner of the thoughts and intents of the heart."* In these last days, it is vital for you to have the Bible in your heart and at your disposal to successfully defeat the spiritual enemies that try to accost your mind.

Action Item #4 - Quickly confess sin, repent and receive the cleansing of Jesus' blood. Be quick to confess sin and receive the cleansing blood of Jesus as part of a plan to build a wall of protection around your life. Many people want the finished work of forgiveness that was accomplished by the substitutionary work of Jesus on the cross, his dying for our sins, and we want the end result of knowing we have been forgiven of our confessed sin, but never repent. What the Alpha and Omega did for you and I on the Cross and what will be eternity is from His love for us. Our part, remember this, is to repent! To do a 180 degree turn away from the sin, the actions, the behaviors, the attitudes, and the pleasures. Turn Away!

There are stubborn sinners and some believers who refuse to apologize, liars who claim to be sorry when they're not, and hypocrites who may truly believe they're sorry yet lack sympathy or understanding of biblical repentance. So, what are the attributes of genuine repentance? Here are eight signs I've gleaned from life and from God's Word.

1. A Repentant Person Is Appalled by Sin

Horrified by what they've done, a repentant person will humble themselves, grieve the pain they've caused, and be cut to the heart in their conviction. As the prophet mourned in Isaiah 6:5, *"Woe to me! I am ruined! For I am a man of unclean lips, and I live among a people of unclean lips."* Isaiah called his mess out. Sin is messy, call it out, confess it. The Psalmist says, *"I have admitted my ways are wrong, and You responded; now help me learn what You require."* (Psalm 119:26 The VOICE Translation)

2. They Make Amends

In Luke 19:1–10, we read the story of Zacchaeus and the generosity he demonstrated as part of his repentance. A tax collector, thief, and oppressor of God's people, Zacchaeus made amends: *"Here and now I give half of my possessions to the poor. And if I have cheated anybody out of anything, I will pay back four times the amount"* (v. 8). And Jesus confirmed the authenticity of Zacchaeus's repentance: *"Today salvation has come to this house"* (v. 9).

3. They Accept Consequences

A genuinely repentant person will accept consequences. These may include losing the trust of others, relinquishing a position of authority, or submitting to worldly authorities such as law enforcement. When the thief on the cross repented, he said to his companion, *"Do you not fear God? . . . We are punished justly, for we are getting what our deeds deserve"* (Luke 23:40–41). And Jesus commended his repentance by assuring him of his salvation: *"Truly I say to you, today you will be with me in paradise"* (Luke 23:43). To get to the place in life, the place in my marriage and family, but more to be where I am with my relationship with the Lord, I've had to walk the road of consequences, considering not my own reputation or ego.

4. They Don't Expect or Demand Forgiveness

Often, I've been told by my abuser, "If you don't forgive me, God won't forgive you." But this threatening posture indicates insincere repentance. It's unloving, manipulative, and implies the offender doesn't accept or comprehend the gravity of what they've done. When Jacob approached Esau and repented, he didn't expect mercy, let alone compassion. In Genesis 32, we read he felt "great fear" and "distress" (v. 7). He anticipated an attack (v. 11) and considered himself unworthy of kindness (v. 10). In fact, so certain was Jacob of retribution that he separated his wives, children, and servants from him, lest Esau's anger fall on them too.

5. They Feel the Depth of the Pain They've Caused

A repentant person won't try to minimize, downplay, or excuse what they've done. They won't point to all their good works as if those actions somehow outweigh or cancel out the bad. They'll view even their "righteous acts" as "filthy rags" (Isa. 64:6). They won't shame the offended party for being hurt or angry. They won't blame their victims or other people for making them sin. Rather, they'll take responsibility, acknowledge the damage they've done, and express remorse.

6. They Change Their Behavior

A truly repentant person will realize they need God to sanctify their heart. They'll proactively work to change their behavior and take steps to avoid sin and temptation. That may mean seeing a counselor, going to rehab, or asking friends, pastors, or law enforcement to give them oversight and hold them accountable. Consider the stark contrast between the church persecutor Saul before salvation and after. Acts 9 tells us that even though some Christians were understandably hesitant to trust him, his character had already altered dramatically.

7. They Allow Space to Heal

The fruit of the Spirit includes patience, kindness, grace, and self-control (Gal. 5:22–23). A truly repentant person will demonstrate these consistently. They won't feel entitled to trust or acceptance; rather, they'll be humble, unassuming, and willing to sacrifice their own wants and needs for the benefit of the injured party. They won't pressure someone to hurry up and "get over it" or "move on." Rather, they'll understand our distrust, acknowledge our grief, and honor the boundaries we've requested.

8. They are in Awe by Forgiveness

If a person feels entitled to forgiveness, they don't value forgiveness. When Jacob received Esau's forgiveness, he was so astounded he wept: *"To see your face is like seeing the face of God, for you have received me favorably"* (Gen. 30:10). Jacob realized that forgiveness is a divine miracle, a picture of the Messiah, and a sign of the Lord's mercy. Though Jacob and Esau hadn't spoken for 40 years, Jacob knew God had enabled Esau, by grace, to forgive him.

We all make mistakes, some unintentional and some intentional. Regardless of why, as soon as you awaken to the fact that you've done or thought something that is inappropriate, learn to quickly act on First John 1:9. It says, *"If we confess our sins, He is faithful and just to forgive us of our sins and to cleanse us from all unrighteousness."*

Proverbs 28:13 says, *"He that covereth his sins shall not prosper: but whoso confesseth and forsaketh them shall have mercy."* When we ignore or try to hide sin, it negatively clogs our spiritual lives and makes us susceptible to attacks of the enemy. But quickly confessing sin and submitting to the cleansing power of Jesus' blood keeps us free of self-condemnation and keeps our hearts pliable.

Don't let your heart become hardened by allowing unconfessed sin to build in your soul. By quickly confessing sin and submitting to the cleansing power of Jesus' blood, you'll receive forgiveness and mercy, and it will help your soul stay free in these last days. You will quickly receive cleansing for those things that are inappropriate. Doing this will keep you spiritually free.

Action Item #5 – Commune and receive help from the Holy Spirit. Jesus said, in John14:16-17 *"And I will pray the Father, and he shall give you another Comforter, that he may abide with you for ever; Even the Spirit of truth; whom the world cannot receive,* *because it seeth him not, neither knoweth him: but ye know him; for he dwelleth with you, and shall be in you."*

In the original Greek, Jesus was saying, I am sending you a counselor, a helper, an advocate. Be honest with yourself right here. How many times have you said a quick prayer about decisions and/or circumstances and then moved right into going about things your way? Without asking and seeking help from Holy Spirit. Let's change that moving forward. Commune and receive help from Holy Spirit. Remember Hebrews 4:16, *"Let us therefore come boldly unto the throne of grace, that we may obtain mercy, and find grace to help in time of need."*

Action Item #6 – Make a covenant with your eyes. Make a covenant with your eyes as part of a plan to build a wall of protection around your life. Psalm 101:3 says, *"I will set no wicked thing before mine eyes...."* Evil often finds access into your mind and imagination through your eyes.

Matthew 6:22 says, *"Your eye is like a lamp that provides light for your body. When your eye is healthy, your whole body is filled with light"* (NLT). If your eyes are focused on what is healthy, it will bring good things into your mind. But if your eyes are focused on what is unhealthy or foul, those vile things will enter your mind and affect you negatively. An ancient saying tells us "the eye is the window to the soul." Though this saying is not found in the Bible, it is true that your eyes are the gateway to your mind, imagination, and to what positively or negatively affects your thinking.

We are living in the last days, and that means we are living in an environment where wicked things — especially sexually lewd images — are constantly being put on display before our eyes. To stop those images from entering your mind and thus allowing the devil to have a tool to use against you, it is essential that you make a covenant with your eyes — a covenant that you will not give permission for any wicked thing to be displayed before your eyes.

Action Item #7 - Maintain a relationship with those to whom you are spiritually accountable. You need a relationship with those to whom you are spiritually accountable as part of a plan to build a wall of protection around your life. This is more than attending church or being a member of a church. Are you in fellowship and covenant with a church? Do they know you? Are you known among the body? Your past, your temperament, your relationships, are you all doing life together? Proverbs 11:14 says, *"Where no counsel is, the people fall: but in the multitude of counsellors there is safety."* And Proverbs 24:6 reiterates, *"...In a multitude of counsellors there is safety."* According to these verses, a person who has godly counselors in his or her life is a wise person.

The fact is that everyone needs someone to whom he or she is spiritually accountable and to whom he or she can turn for counsel in time of need. That person could be your pastor, or it could be someone whose spiritual maturity is beyond yours, whose counsel you respect — someone who is trusted, confidential, and mature.

In Psalm 54:4, David said, *"Behold, God is mine helper: the Lord is with them that uphold my soul."* Who do you have in your life that strengthens you and your soul? You need people in your life to give you strength, who will speak into your life and who will watch out for your soul. You need them to be honest with you, pray with you, speak the truth of the Word to you and hold you accountable. This is healthy for you, especially in these last days when the enemy is waging extensive warfare against our souls.

By having such a person (or persons) in your life — one with whom you can talk and confide — a safety net is provided to help you in times of need and to keep you strong. As David said, you need those who "strengthen your soul" especially during these last days when many will be tempted to fall into various temptations.

Action Item #8 - Regularly attend a church that teaches from the Bible. You need to attend a church where you will be encouraged from the Bible as part of a plan to build a wall of protection around your life. Psalm 119:28 marvelously depicts the powerful effect of

God's Word to divinely energize a person who otherwise would feel physically or emotionally weak. In fact, when the psalmist was confronted with his own humanity, he knew that the Word would strengthen him to rise above it. That's why he said, *"...Strengthen thou me according unto thy word."*

The role of the Bible cannot be underestimated in your life. In fact, the amount of spiritual fire you have burning at your core is directly related to how much of God's Word is planted in your heart. Within the covers of the Bible are all the answers for every problem you will ever face. The Bible can bring new life to your heart, establish order in your mind, and refresh your soul when it is being rocked by emotions.

When you hear the Scriptures expounded by the anointing of the Holy Spirit, or when you read the Bible to take it by faith into your heart, its supernatural power is *unleashed.* And when that happens, your heart, your will, your thoughts, your emotions and memories are all touched by God's power. Satan knows the life-transforming power that is locked inside the Bible. That's why he fights so hard to get believers and churches to back away from it. He lures them to water it down, modify it, or even eliminate it.

So, I want to ask — are you attending a church where the emphasis is on a solid foundation of biblical truth? We are living in the last of the last days, and you need the spiritual strength and the camaraderie of a church that is committed to His Word!

Action #9 - Walk In Obedience. The lone, simple act of obedience to the Word of God will without fail, produce powerful results. Samuel's understanding of obedience allowed God do for him what God desires to do for all who are faithful to His Word. The Bible explains why Samuel was feared as one of the greatest Prophets who ever lived, *"And Samuel grew, and the LORD was with him, and did let none of his words fall to the ground."* (1 Samuel 3:19)

Whatever Samuel said, God would make sure that it came to pass. It was the Prophet's grasp on the principle of submission and obedience that enabled him to walk in a place of great spiritual authority. You must learn to walk in obedience and submission to the Word and will of God for your life. You can do it!

Samuel tried to teach King Saul this principle but to no avail. Hear his words: *"...Hath the LORD as great delight in burnt offerings and sacrifices, as in obeying the voice of the LORD? Behold, to obey is better than sacrifice, and to hearken than the fat of rams"* (1 Samuel 15:22). Obedience is the life-giving force that resurrects dead faith. The act of obeying adds works to faith bringing it to life and living faith pleases God (See James 2:20, Hebrews 11:6). The Apostle James basically teaches the essentiality of acting on the Word of God in order to produce positive spiritual results in life. By taking action and being a doer of the Word, the promises of God become a reality of life. Simple obedience to God's Word by consistently praying early each morning will give life to many promises and blessings. The promises and blessings of God will begin to be manifest in the lives of those who practice submission and obedience.

I declare over your life that:

1. What the devil (and the giants) thought they were using to destroy your life, God is going to manufacture and work out of the same attack and evil; good.
2. I declare He is going to promote you and change your mess into a message and your test into a testimony.
3. Stop worrying about what the devil, your giants, or people are doing; look to the bigger picture, there is a purpose for your giant.
4. Don't faint, don't give up, soon you will see why God has allowed all this to happen to you.
5. I declare that this is your moment of revelation, where your enemies are brought to shame and you are brought to fame in Jesus name. THEY WERE TO BE CONQUERED AND UTTERLY DESTROYED AS THEY WERE HEATHEN (EVIL): these nations/giants were not in the

covenant; they represented a snare.

Chapter 12

Epilogue:
To the Victor Goes the Spoils, The Spoils of Victory

Some of you may have at some point asked the question why a title a book "A Fight Worth Having"? What makes it worth it? The answer is simple; becoming a giant slayer makes life exhilarating, exciting and victorious. Victory taste good! Victory smells good! Victory feels good. There is nothing like victory after a battle, a fight, a war, or a struggle. As a child, on Saturdays I use to love watching ABC Sports on television. Particularly the boxing events. The late sports announcer, Jim McKay who passed away in 2008, was best known for hosting <u>ABC's Wide World of Sports</u> (1961–1998). His introduction for that program has passed into American Pop Culture: "Spanning the globe to bring you the constant variety of sports... the thrill of victory... and the agony of defeat... the human drama of athletic competition..."

At the end of a fight, a war, a battle and a struggle, there is a winner! Coming out victorious has many benefits. There are trophies, grand prize money, the significance of having your name remembered as a champion! Something tangible comes after all the pain, struggle and agony. For you my sisters and brothers, there will never be anything like coming out on the other side victorious over the giants who were designed to defeat you. Isaiah 54:17 says, *"No weapon formed against you shall prosper, And every tongue which rises against you in judgment You shall condemn. This is the heritage of the servants of the LORD, And their righteousness is from Me, Says the LORD."*

During a Congressional debate in 1831 a New York senator, William L. Marcy, used the phrase "to the victor belong the spoils." This saying accurately described the spoils system of appointing government workers. Each time a new political administration comes into power thousands of public servants are discharged and members of the victorious political party take over their jobs.

This is the season of the Giant Slayer and to the VICTOR goes the SPOILS. For all the hell and pain you have walked through, you now get to take over the very thing that tried to take you over and take you out. For every victory you have achieved, don't you dare walk away without the spoils! Through every danger, every toil, every snare, every heartache, every tear drop, every sleepless night, every counseling session, every prayer, every fast, every headache, every mistake, every failure, every embarrassment; it cost you something, so take possession of the spoils of victory. If it is your peace of mind that you now enjoy; if it is the stability of your finances; if like myself it is a loving and stable marriage and family life, if it is the joy of the Lord you walk in, if it is your divine health, if it is a prodigal son's return or prodigal daughter's return home, whether it's your business bouncing back; whatever it is, give God praise and glory and enjoy the spoils of victory!

Spoils of war are defined as "any profits extracted as the result of winning a war or other military activity." According to 50 USCS § 2204 [Title 50. War and National Defense; Chapter 39. Spoils of War], *spoils of war mean enemy movable property lawfully captured, seized, confiscated, or found which has become United States property in accordance with the laws of war.*

The first mention of spoils of war, in the Bible is in connection with the conquest of Sodom and Gomorrah. Genesis 14:8-12, *"Then the king of Sodom, the king of Gomorrah, the king of Admah, the king of Zeboiim, and the king of Bela (that is, Zoar) went out and lined up for battle in the Valley of Siddim against Chedorlaomer king of Elam, Tidal king of Goiim, Amraphel king of Shinar, and Arioch king of Ellasar—four kings against five. Now the Valley of Siddim contained many asphalt pits, and [as] the kings of Sodom and Gomorrah fled, [some] fell into them, but the rest fled to the mountains. The [four kings] took all the goods of Sodom and Gomorrah and all their food and went on. They also took Abram's nephew Lot and his possessions, for he was living in Sodom, and they went on."*

Abraham (Abram at the time) went after the invaders because they had taken his nephew, Lot, as their prisoner. He defeated them and recovered all the spoils. Actually verse 16 says these words, *"And he brought back all the goods."*

Let's also look at 2 Chronicles 20 where Jehoshaphat was at war with the Moabites and the Ammonites. In reading, preaching and teaching on this we spend a lot of time reminding people of verse 15, *"that the battle is not yours, it's the Lords,"* and yes, that is true. However, this is the season of the Giant Slayer and to the victor go the spoils. So, when we read down further in chapter 20, we come across a mind-blowing occurrence about how long it took Jehoshaphat and the people to gather the spoils!

> 2 Chronicles 20:25
> *"And when Jehoshaphat and his people came to take away the spoil of them, they found among them in abundance both riches with the dead bodies, and precious jewels, which they stripped off for themselves, more than they could carry away:* **and they were three days in gathering of the spoil, it was so much."**

Three days gathering the spoils! Let that sink in. You are about to enjoy a season where you will be able to take your time in taking the spoils, of taking back the goods. The reference and mentioning of how long it took Jehoshaphat and his people to gather the spoils of victory is not a wasted mention. It speaks to taking the time to gather, process and take home the spoils. I encourage and exhort you my sisters and brothers that you take the time to gather, process, and take home the spoils of a hard-fought victory.

How do you enjoy the spoils of being delivered? By walking in your newfound liberty and deliverance. What exactly does that look like? Paul lays out a case for grace and liberty/freedom in Galatians 5:1, *"Stand fast therefore in the liberty wherewith Christ hath made us free, and be not entangled again with the yoke of bondage."* In other words, I have no intention of going back to what I defeated! I'm not going back to what I slain and killed, its dead to me. Say it out loud, write in in your journal, tweet it, shout it, I'm not going back!

Legalists and law-mongers attack the gospel of grace and accuse those that rejoice in the liberty that we have in Christ's finished work at Calvary. As a dangerous doctrine, that leads to a carnal lifestyle and a license to sin.

However, this is a serious misunderstanding of the gospel of grace and a gross misinterpretation of the apostolic teachings of Paul - who was Christ's chosen apostle to the gentiles and through whom we're given the marvelous mysteries of the Church - which is His body.

Paul taught that this treasured freedom we have in Christ is ours by grace through faith in Him. It is this very liberty that we have in Christ's finished work at Calvary, which has released us from our former legalistic yoke of bondage, set us free from the curse of the Law, and freed us from all addictions, giants, and so on.

God's perfect Law demanded an unattainable standard of moral perfection and an outward display of disciplined living, but we fall short of that perfect standard that God requires. We all have need of a Savior who is willing to pay the price for our sin. For this reason, Christ came to fulfill the Law on our behalf. Christ lived a perfect life so that He could attain to God's perfect standard on our behalf. He then chose to pay the price for our sins so that by faith we might be made the righteousness of God - in Him.

In order to pay the price for our sin He died in our place. But having lived a perfect life that was not deserving of death, God raised Him from the dead and highly exalted Him - so that all who believe on Him would not perish but have life, eternal life. His resurrected life within. His new, born-again life. 'Our new man in Christ, who has been created in God's image,' - and this is the testimony, that God gave us eternal life, and this life is in his Son.

Christian liberty is not a dangerous doctrine as the legalists and law-mongers would have us believe. Legalism seeks to change the old sin nature from the outside and force it to obey God's perfect, unachievable Law in our own strength - but it fails every time.

The surrendered believer, who is walking in spirit and in truth, is yielded to the guidance of the indwelling Holy Spirit, who works through our new life in Christ. Over time we discover an inner discipline at work. The spirit-filled Christian discovers the righteous requirements of God's law being fulfilled in and through him.

How wonderful to discover this godly liberty we have in Christ who has set us free from the yoke of bondage, by means of the indwelling Holy Spirit who is working in us day by day, transforming our new life in Christ, into the image and likeness of the Lord Jesus Christ. May we stand fast in this liberty wherewith Christ hath made us free and be not entangled again with the legalistic yoke of bondage.

The greatest spoil of all took place at the Cross.

"Having spoiled principalities and powers, he made a shew of them openly, triumphing over them in it" (Colossians 2:15).

Jesus plundered; He took back things that Satan had no legal authority to have. The devil at Calvary, stripping him of all power and authority. When Christ rose victorious from the grave, he led an innumerable host of redeemed captives out of Satan's grasp. And that blood-bought procession is still marching on. Yet, amazingly, Christ's triumph at Calvary gave us even more than victory over death. It gained for us incredible spoils in this life: grace, mercy, peace, forgiveness, strength, faith, and freedom; everything needed to lead an overcoming life.

So, your enjoyment of freedom is much more important to God than many of the day-to-day decisions that fill us with so much concern. A good test of your priorities in life would be whether you are just as concerned about the command to enjoy your freedom as you are about other pressing decisions in your life. Do you exercise as much diligence in prayer and study to stand fast in freedom as you do to decide about home, job, school, and marriage partner? It is a clear and unqualified command: *"Stand fast and do not submit again to a yoke of slavery."* This is the will of God for you: your freedom. Uncompromising, unrelenting, indomitable freedom. For this Christ died. For this he rose. For this he sent his Spirit. There is nothing He wills with more intensity under the glory of his own name than this: your freedom.

I want you to open your mouth now and declare that;

- I refuse to believe the lie of the giants or any enemy I encounter.
- I choose to fight the good fight of faith.
- I am not going to die in my wilderness.
- I will possess my promised land/my life of victory.
- I am going to fight until I WIN!
- I am going to enjoy the freedom Christ won for me and extends to me.

How bad do you want victory? If you want it bad enough:

IT'S A FIGHT WORTH HAVING!

Bibliography

1. Unless otherwise noted, all scripture references are from King James Version
2. Aliens and Fallen Angels by Stephen Quayle
3. Alien Intrusion by Gary Bates Alien
4. Encounters by Chuck Missler and Mark Eastman
5. Apollyon Rising 2012 by Thomas Horn www.beforeus.com
6. Companion Bible King James Version by E.W. Bullinger
7. http://www.biblebelievers.org.au/giants.htm
8. www.bible.ca
9. http://biblefacts.org/myth/giant2.html
10. http://bibleprobe.com/nephilim.htm
11. Bible Student's Commentary by G. Ch. Aalders
12. http://www.bibliotecapleyades.net/vida_alien/alien_watchers10.htm
13. The Book of Enoch by Enoch
14. Book of Jasher by Jasher
15. The Giants of Noah's Day by Stanley Price
16. Giants-the Mystery and the Myth by Discovery Channel
17. Giants: Sons of the Gods, Douglas Van Dorn, 2013 published by Water of Creation
18. My Utmost for His Highest, Oswald Chambers. Our Daily Bread Publishing; Revised, Updated Language Edition (July 3, 2017)
19. The Mighty "ITES" Before You (Israel) & Your Destiny, Hlopho Phamodi
20. The Proper Names of the Old Testament Expounded, W.A. Jones
21. The Amplified Bible Classic Edition (AMPC)
22. The Self-Esteem Workbook, Glenn R. Schiraldi, PhD,, New Harbinger Publications; Second Edition, Revised November 1, 2016
23. Cambridge Dictionary 1999 Cambridge University Press has

been publishing dictionaries for learners of English since 1995.

24. Weymouth Bible October 26, 2018
25. Conybeare Pauls Letters Translation 1872
26. Moffatt Bible Kregel Classics; 2 Reprintnd Edition (April 28, 2004)
27. Revised Standard Bible American Bible Society (June 1, 1997)
28. Phillips Modern English Bible J. B. Phillips New Testament in Modern English – May 8, 2009
29. New Living Translation Tyndale, Mar 1, 2006
30. 2013 Title 50 USCS § 2204 War and National Defense; Chapter 39. Spoils of War
31. Statistics on Christian Giving is from ChristianUnion.org
32. The Positive Psychology Practitioner's Toolkit, https://positivepsychology.com/toolkit/
33. The Feeling Good Handbook, Plume; Revised Edition May 1, 1999

About the Author

Prophet Delavago Scruggs was born in Philadelphia, PA, raised in Washington, DC, and gave his life to Jesus Christ on December 24, 1976.

Prophet Delavago comes from a line of Kingdom- and global-impacting preachers of the Gospel. His late grandfather, Rev. George B. Wilson, uniquely pastored churches in the Baptist, Methodist and Presbyterian denominations. His great-uncle, the late Apostle Quander Wilson, the founder and Presiding Prelate of the Greater Emmanuel Apostolic Churches was a pioneer in connecting believers and churches across denominational lines. Prophet was raised in the home of Archbishop Alfred A. Owens, Jr. and Dr. Susie T. Owens, where he learned the foundational truths of the Kingdom and the value of education.

For over 40 years, Prophet Delavago has carried the gospel to over 25 states and abroad, pastored 2 churches, undergirded several ministries, and laid the foundation of several Bible institutes, leading one to full national accreditation. He is a noted Bible teacher, and previously authored a book entitled, *"Battle of Bended Knee, A Prayer Manual"* (currently out of print).

Prophet Delavago has a special grace for men's ministry. In

recent years, he founded and graduated two classes of The Bethesda Men's Group, which is a 12-week problem-solving group designed to help men examine unconfronted issues in their lives and openly discuss how to walkout a healed and victorious life.

Prophet Delavago has a BA degree from American University and has completed graduate coursework at Oral Roberts University and the University of the District of Columbia. Over the last 20 years, his career journey has led him to serve as a national subject matter expert for various non-profit, faith- and community-based organizations.

Prophet is married to his partner in life, ministry and business, Pastor Aretha Scruggs. They recently launched a training and consulting company, Until We All, to help ministry and community leaders fulfill their God-given purpose and mission. They also serve as associate pastors of Kingdom Celebration Center in Gambrills MD, under the leadership of Apostle Antonio and Pastor Barbara Palmer, and share the blessing of 5 children and 4 grandchildren.

PROPHET

Delavago Scruggs